parent
on
purpose

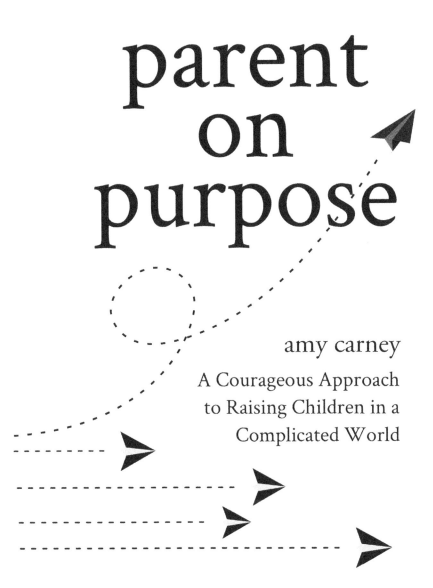

parent on purpose

amy carney

A Courageous Approach
to Raising Children in a
Complicated World

Niche Pressworks
Indianapolis

Parent on Purpose

ISBN: 978-1-946533-34-0 Paperback

Copyright © 2019 by Amy Carney

Unless otherwise noted, all Scripture quotations are taken from the New American Standard Bible (NASB), Copyright 1975 by Nelson Publishers.

For permission to reprint portions of this content or bulk purchases, contact Amy Carney at www. AmyCarney.com

Published by Niche Pressworks, Indianapolis, IN

NichePressworks.com

Printed in the United States of America

For other queries, contact amy@amycarney.com.

To Keith.
For always believing in me and loving us all so well.

And to our dear children.
It's a privilege to raise each of you.
May you always be blessed and be a blessing.

Contents

Foreword

Parenting is in a state of shambles in America. Children have not changed over the past forty years. In fact, today's kids bring the same nature into the world that kids brought with them into the world four thousand years ago. Obviously, then, they are not the problem. What has changed over the past forty years is child rearing.

There was a time in America, and not so long ago, when the raising of children was done casually and matter-of-factly, a time when parents possessed strong confidence in the legitimacy of their authority. During that same time, children were mischievous, but except in very rare instances, they were not belligerently disobedient or disrespectful. In school, they did their best without much parental help at all, and they managed to behave themselves without medication. By the time children were three, toddlerhood had ended. Tantrums and defiance had stopped. Children entertained themselves, did not interrupt adults and did not ask for much adult attention.

In the mid-to-late 1960s, American parents began listening to psychologists (of which I am one), and other mental health professionals tell them how to properly rear children. Rather rapidly, a legacy of knowledge and common sense was replaced with psychological theory, and things began going, as my mother would have put it, "to hell in a handbasket." Today, the mental health of children is a major cultural issue, the behavior of many children is out-of-control and "parenting" as we now call it has become something stressful and anxiety-arousing.

It's evident that we cannot continue down this destructive path, but what can parents do?

For starters, moms and dads can begin doing as this book suggests—parent on purpose.

I am delighted to write this foreword, because Amy Carney and I share the same determination to transform the way people raise children, one household at a time. Amy and I both know that what we teach through our writing and speaking is not original but based on solid Biblical truths.

Purposeful parenting has been the focus of my writing and speaking for over twenty-five years. I have a weekly syndicated column in over 200 newspapers nationwide, and I have written 15 best-selling books on the subject. I am delighted that Amy has added this much-needed book to the conversation.

Amy's simple message about parenting on purpose is not new, but it is timely and needed in today's culture. Her book reminds parents of the importance of slowing down and claiming their parenting goals, so they can better lead, love, and launch their child successfully.

Not only is Amy passionate about raising her own five children purposefully in (or despite) popular culture today, but her passion spills over into helping others understand how to lovingly regain leadership in their home while relaxing into their God-given role as a parent.

Amy has written a book that illuminates a path to the end of full-time parenthood. I think you will find it helpful how each of the nine chapters begins with a specific problem parents face today and is then followed up by solutions and strategies to help you strengthen your parental leadership, your family culture, and the child you are currently raising. The goal of *Parent on Purpose* is to help moms and dads walk a more intentional journey today so that when they arrive at the finish line of full-time parenthood, they feel joy and peace instead of guilt and regret.

I would suggest that you read the book a little at a time and slowly begin to integrate Amy's suggestions. Whether you have a newborn or you are about to venture into the teenage years, this thoughtful book will help you obtain a strong finish to your season of child-rearing. If you follow the commonsense advice contained in her work, you will not only transform your life but that of your child and therefore the world around you. If you've lost your way and claimed the wrong goals while raising your child, *Parent on Purpose* will guide you home.

John Rosemond
www.JohnRosemond.com

Introduction

The Decision That Changed Everything

In 2014, my husband Keith and I bought a motorhome, packed up our twelve-year-old triplet sons and eleven-year-old daughter, said goodbye to our carefully constructed Phoenix lifestyle, and left to travel around the United States.

Why would we do such a thing?

Because we had to.

On the surface, life couldn't have appeared more successful. There were A's on the kids' report cards; trophies on the shelves; and money in the bank. Yet, underneath this facade of worldly success, our family was disconnected and drifting apart.

We claimed one reality yet lived another. Our children were accomplished and achieved at a high level while we funded their opportunities and shuttled them around. We rarely gathered around the dinner table or sat together in a church pew. Although Keith and I said faith and family were priorities, our calendars told a different story. We consistently divided and conquered life apart from one another. With kids in various activities, Keith and I continually sat, separately, on the sidelines of our children's lives cheering them on until one day we woke up to the fact that we were growing apart as a couple and as a family, and we needed to make a change.

We had allowed popular culture to dictate our family narrative. I had wanted to cultivate a more connected family than the one I grew up in, yet how could that ever be possible when we didn't even spend much time together? I wanted my children to grow up in an outward focused home with God at the helm, yet our priorities served ourselves rather than Jesus.

Though it was scary, we knew that bravely saying yes to this RV adventure was precisely the medicine our disconnected family needed. So, Keith sacrificed his position as player development coach for the Chicago Blackhawks. We pulled our kids out of their public-school classrooms and off of their club sports teams, and we resigned from our organized activities. We said goodbye to our friends and life as we knew it, and, for over half a year, our family bonded our way around forty-four states. It was a journey that strengthened our disjointed family and changed our perspectives on parenting.

My blog followers, friends, and family encouraged me to write a book about our adventures, so I began writing this narrative about what I thought you'd want to know regarding touring around our beautiful country. I planned to tell you about the friendly town of Lava Hot Springs, Idaho, and how you should visit the covered bridges of Quechee, Vermont, in the fall. I was going to write about our stay at the unique sheep farm in Montana and about the natural waterslide our kids went down over and over again in Asheville, North Carolina.

But, as I began to write these stories, I realized that this wasn't what I wanted to share with you. I'd already written about our experiences and the places we visited on my blog, so I no longer wanted this book to be about where to take your kids or the best routes to get there.

I realized that what I wanted to share with you was the heart behind our trip—our why. How we became proactive instead of reactive parents, and how we learned to consciously parent on purpose today to cultivate the legacy that we want to leave behind tomorrow.

Just as our family couldn't travel around the USA without a roadmap and a plan, you and I can't aimlessly lead our families without claiming where in the world we're headed or how we plan to get there.

I've written this book as a reminder that we, as parents, only get one shot at raising a child and cultivating a healthy childhood. We get one chance to take the time and make the effort to influence the people who currently live in our care and under our guidance.

Keith and I will soon launch our triplets and our daughter within one year of each other. I don't want to sit at their high school graduations or at college drop-off feeling sad or regretting that I should have done this or could have done that differently. Instead, I want to embrace the end of full-time parenthood now and make choices today with this inevitable moment in mind.

Parent on Purpose is not about striving to be the perfect mother or father or to raise perfect children. We are imperfect humans raising imperfect little humans. Perfection is never our goal; the objective of this book is to help you become more intentional.

In this book, I share my process of how to better parent on purpose through three simple pillars—LEAD, LOVE, and LAUNCH.

In the first part, LEAD, we will discuss how to strengthen our personal and family identity by taking the time and making the effort to claim who we are, what we believe, and how we can better live what we say to be our truth. In this section, we determine our vision, values, and purpose.

The second part, LOVE, is about purposely strengthening our family relationships by taking the time and making the effort to put down the screens and play more. We'll touch on the importance of developing a unique family culture that is abundant in meaningful traditions and rituals.

Finally, we will talk about how we need to better prepare our child for the LAUNCH into adulthood. We will focus on strengthening our child's life skills and their ability to focus on others rather than just themselves. We will discuss how we can raise hard working, responsible, and empathetic adults.

My hope is that one of the ideas, inspirations, strategies, or stories in here was written just for you. I hope this book inspires you to better parent on purpose today so that you feel more joy and peace raising your child and launching them into the world tomorrow. No matter how many children you have or how many years have already passed, you can pause, pivot, and plan a purposeful course for your family.

Let's parent on purpose today, my friend, while we still can!

PART 1:

LEAD

lead on purpose

PARENT from the end Be proactive *instead of reactive*

 WHERE ARE YOU HEADED?
VISION - **VALUES** - PURPOSE

Take the time MAKE THE EFFORT *author* your story

 Determine your destination
TRANSFER YOUR VALUES
PRIORITIZE YOUR PURPOSE

Mind *the gap*

Childhood *is not a dress rehearsal* AIM FOR adulthood

BUILD YOUR value village

THINK **CHARACTER** OVER COLLEGE

18 YEARS

BE THE EXAMPLE
WALK YOUR TALK
practice what you preach

make *courageous* CHOICES

ACT LIKE THE CEO

Focus on the WHO *instead of the DO*

www.amycarney.com

Chapter 1

Visualize the End

Imagine that your loved ones have gathered. Family members and friends have flown into town. Your tribe has reunited to celebrate your baby who graduates from high school tomorrow. You can't believe you've already arrived at this monumental moment.

How did the time pass so quickly? Tonight's celebration will kick off with a film highlighting your family story over the past eighteen years.

This movie won't be the ordinary five-minute montage that we've all seen before—smiling photos set to a sappy theme song. No, imagine that this flick will be about the actual journey of your family, and what the main character, your graduate, has experienced while living in your home.

The buzz of everyone's excitement will calm as the lights dim, and your family reel begins. You're feeling good, smug even. Hadn't you provided your son with everything he needed and more? Hadn't you pushed him to achieve on every level? Stood up for him in every battle?

Get ready for the eighteen-year adventures of your firstborn. Roll 'em.

The film starts off just fine. What a cute baby! And look, what a loving big brother he was as the siblings came along. But, wait a minute. Who are all of these older ladies you keep passing in the grocery stores advising you to enjoy your children as you stressfully push them through the aisles? "Enjoy them. They grow up fast." Sure, you can see their wisdom now, but you were busy, for goodness sake. What did they know about your life?

The images speed up—this class, that class, this team, that team, dinners in the car, dinners alone, parents split up at various events, kids alone with cell phones, tablets, Netflix, and YouTube. What about that vacation we squeezed in the summer between eighth grade and high school? Oh yeah, there it went.

Hey, slow this film down! We had more together time than this, didn't we? We laughed sometimes. I know we did, yet the scenes are showing a different story.

> BUILDING A STRONG FAMILY AND RAISING A STRONG ADULT ARE BOTH CULTIVATED BY A PURPOSEFUL LEADER WHO TAKES THE TIME AND MAKES AN EFFORT TO TURN A VISION INTO REALITY THROUGH INTENTIONAL ACTION.

You slouch in your seat as you realize that the family story everyone is viewing on the screen isn't unique at all. The audience is stuck watching a childhood consumed with achievements, accomplishments, accolades, and stuff. They watch your family members divided and disconnected, and you realize, suddenly, how ordinary and boring it all seems. Maybe, those strangers in the grocery store were right. Their hindsight was meant to be your insight, but instead, you chose to ignore their truth.

You begin to feel sad. Guilty. Uneasy. Cheated, perhaps. You realize you want to go back and start over, but it's too late. The way you spent that precious time with your family is over. Your firstborn's eighteen-year reel is complete, and he's now ready to leave the security of your home and head into the real world. You break out in a sweat as you realize you want to stop the movie, but you can't because the actual narrative has already played out in real life.

There is no second chance at creating a childhood. You wonder how nearly two decades flew by without you understanding the depth of this precious season.

Until this moment, you hadn't realized that you were actually in charge of authoring this story—that you would be the screenwriter. Why didn't anyone tell you that? Had you understood that, perhaps everyone would have seen a much different story play out on the big screen tonight.

Your head spins as you wonder if you did enough for your child. Or, perhaps, you did too much?

Did you teach your son the things that will sustain him as an adult living in the real world? Did you create enough meaningful moments during his childhood to keep him connected to family relationships while he is gone?

The film ends, and you wish with all of your heart that you had begun your parenting journey with this film in mind.

In today's culture, a strong family story doesn't happen by accident, and neither does raising a strong adult. Both are cultivated by a purposeful leader who takes the time and makes an effort to turn a vision into reality through intentional action. Our goal, as parents, is to get to that movie theater to celebrate our high school graduate and feel joyful watching his childhood story unfold on the big screen. Our job is to take our eighteen-year screenwriting journey seriously.

WHAT'S THE PROBLEM?

Screenwriters begin writing their script with the end in mind so that they can stay focused on how they want the story to turn out. When we know the end goal, as a screenwriter or a parent, we can better create the scenes that will lead the characters in our story to the desired ending. If we just cruise along, reactively writing the narrative as we go, we will most likely be surprised when the ending sneaks up on us and looks nothing like we had intended.

What keeps us from proactively parenting and living out the stories we really want to tell in the end?

The problem starts with the cereal aisle in our local mega-grocery store. Can you say overwhelming? Why do we need over 130 varieties of boxed breakfast cereals to decide between? Back in the day, there was one yellow box of ordinary Cheerios. Now, there are at least thirteen flavors of that brand to choose from.

In America, we are bombarded with too many choices in every aspect of our lives. Our culture has complicated everything, from cereal choices to parenthood. It's no wonder we're confused, stressed, and overwhelmed when raising children today. We don't know which way we're supposed to turn. So, rather than taking the time to figure it out, we just continue in our daily routine, tackling what's put in front of us because it appears to matter the most.

We jump into raising a child and mistakenly spend nearly two decades tackling the urgent, disguised as important. Our daily calendars and checklists distract us from fully grasping the fact that the finish line of full-time parenthood is looming ahead. We forget that the child we are raising today is indeed going to grow up and leave us, even though this is, and has been, the goal for all parents since the beginning of time. Yet, it is all too common today to hear parents express surprise that this phase of life has already come to an end.

Not long ago, as I patiently stood in line to pick up my photos at Costco, I noticed the woman in front of me staring intently at the high school graduation announcement in her hand. In my boredom and desire to connect with another adult human, I thought I'd share in her excitement and said, "How awesome. Is that your handsome son?"

I was not expecting her to turn around, with her eyes full of tears and regret, as she said, "Yes. But, no one tells you that one day they are going to grow up and leave you." And without hesitation, I replied, "Yes, they do. But we just don't want to believe it."

The mother (at this moment) had forgotten the goal was to launch her child and was now feeling some remorse. Perhaps she felt she hadn't spent enough time with her son. Or, maybe she felt that she hadn't invested enough in herself while raising him, so she was afraid to face the reality of being without him. It's hard to know what exactly her regrets stemmed from. When faced with my children's high school graduation announcements, I hope that the sadness I'll feel about the end of their childhoods is counterbalanced by an equal amount of joy and peace, knowing that I did my best to launch them into adulthood. This story makes me contemplate what I can do now that will make me feel positive emotions rather than negative ones when I put my full-time parenting role to rest.

God willing, our children will grow up and move into adulthood, as is the natural progression in life. Like it or not, this is an inevitable fact of parenthood. Our particular family reality is that our triplet sons, and subsequently our daughter, will leave our full-time care within one year of each other. As quickly as our foursome entered our home, they will depart from it.

As parents, our "job" is to help our children successfully separate from us at the age of majority and transition into the real world on their own.

I should have told my Costco counterpart not to fret because the chances of her son moving back in with her are pretty good. According to the US Census Bureau, more young adults live in their parents' home than ever before. One in three young people, or about twenty-four million eighteen to thirty-four-year-olds, lived in their parents' home in 2015. Of young people living in their parents' home, one in four are idle—they neither go to school nor work. This figure represents about 2.2 million twenty-five to thirty-four-year-olds.

Given the attention paid to the "boomerang generation" that has "failed to launch," it is surprising that Americans don't rate living independently as a more significant step toward adulthood. Only a quarter of Americans today think that moving out of their parents' home is a vital part of adulthood. This is a problem.

The Carney children fully know that moving out of their childhood home is a prerequisite for adulthood. That's not to say that they might need to move home for a brief period of time. But the point is that children must grow up with an understanding that living independently is a perk of adulthood, not a curse. If we never have conversations with our older children about our expectations of them moving out one day, we can't be surprised when they are still living in our basement much longer than we ever intended.

Perhaps you have heard about the lawsuit Christina and Mark Rotondo filed against their thirty-year-old son. They wanted him to move out and get a job but had to take him to court to evict him from their New York family home. Their son, Michael, said that he felt it was "really unfair" that he didn't get time to plan a "good move." It's evident that this man should have been taught much earlier that life, in fact, can be unfair, and that the perks of childhood must come to an end long before the age of thirty. This case is extreme, but a prime example of what can happen when parents have no end vision and

> **AS PARENTS, OUR "JOB" IS TO HELP OUR CHILDREN SUCCESSFULLY SEPARATE FROM US AT THE AGE OF MAJORITY AND TRANSITION INTO THE REAL WORLD ON THEIR OWN.**

don't properly lead their young adults, or themselves, with the imminent launch in mind.

My teenagers continuously say how unfair it is that they can't have this or can't do that. I tell them to add whatever it is to their ever-growing list of things they can make happen when they move out of our house into adulthood. Childhood is the perfect time for our sons and daughters to get used to the bumps and bruises that unfortunately come with living in the real world. Better that children learn to roll with the punches now instead of being surprised by them later.

WHAT'S THE SOLUTION?

Aim for Adulthood

There's no need to guess where we're headed when raising our children. No matter how we decide to play out the details of our family stories, you and I are parenting toward the same goal: adulthood.

Would you ever jump in a rowboat and head down a river without oars, allowing the current to take you wherever it may? I don't think so, yet this is precisely what we are doing when we jump into parenthood without determining an overarching vision. Instead of intentionally paddling ourselves toward our desired destination, we drift along to wherever popular culture decides to take us, which is most likely not where we want to go.

Stop drifting and claim adulthood as the destination for parenting your child today. Get in your boat, pick up the oars, and purposefully paddle your family toward launch day.

STRATEGIES TO CONSIDER

Parent Six Years Forward

Childhood is not a dress rehearsal, and if you are reading this book, then most likely, the production is well underway. Wherever you may find yourself on the parenthood journey, stop and visualize the day you will launch your child into adulthood.

Now, let's breakdown childhood into three six-year seasons. From zero to six years old is the protection season, when it can be tough to do much more than caretake and survive most days. In the middle, we have what I call our primetime season, when raising children between the ages of seven and twelve. The final season, the preparation years, encompasses ages thirteen to eighteen.

What season is your firstborn in now? Claim that, and then parent ahead to the next season. If your child is in preschool, figure out what you will be facing in elementary school. If your child is in elementary school, look at what parents are dealing with in middle school. And so on and so forth—keep looking ahead!

The good thing is, whether you are currently raising a toddler or a teenager, your screenplay is still in progress. You have time to pause, pivot, and plan for changes that you want and need to make.

Define Your Parenting Purpose
#parentinggoals

Companies have mission statements and manifestos to help them stay focused on their purpose, so why shouldn't we, as parents, create one to help our family stay on a purposeful course.

A manifesto stating who we are, what we believe, and why we believe it to be true will help us lead our family from a proactive state. I call this manifesto a parenting purpose statement. It spells out—*This is us. This is who we are. This is what we do and why we do it.*

No one in your family should ever wonder what you stand for or what your beliefs, goals, values, and expectations are.

A parenting purpose statement helps us define what we desire and hope for when raising our children. It is a personal road map to help you proactively make decisions based on your family priorities and purpose.

Get clear on the end goal for raising your child by starting with what it is that you don't want. Knowing what I don't want has helped me figure out what exactly it is that I do want while raising my children.

Claim What You Don't Want:

- I don't want a family who …
- I don't want to raise children who …
- I don't want to launch adults who …
- I don't want a home where …

Now, Claim What You Do Want:

- I want a family who …
- I want to raise children who …
- I want to launch adults who …
- I want a home where …

If we, as parents, don't take the time to get clear on our desires, we will spend the journey raising our children in reaction to what happens around us in the day to day, stuck in the urgent disguising itself as important.

Let your parenting purpose statement reflect what you believe and help you make courageous choices and decisions based on what you've claimed.

GET STARTED TODAY!

As parents, one of the most important things we can do is regularly evaluate our family priorities and if we are truly living life in accordance with what we say and believe to be important. Is there a gap between what you desire and your current reality?

Pause

What is your present reality?

Envision being in that movie theater tonight watching your firstborn's narrative on the big screen. What makes you happy about what's played out thus far? What makes you feel regret? How do you want to feel as your full-time parenting role comes to an end?

Pivot

What do you want to keep the same? What do you want to do differently?

What would it look like for you to take your parenting journey more seriously? What changes do you now want to make as a result of seeing where you are and knowing that adulthood is your destination?

Plan

What action can you take to move things in the direction you want to go?

Take the time and make the effort to write your parenting purpose statement. What do you want your young adult armored with as they face life on their own without you? What lessons do you want to instill, and how will you go about doing so?

Want guidance creating your parenting purpose statement? Turn to Appendix A where I share how Keith and I wrote ours.

NEXT UP: PARENTS, WE MUST PURPOSELY LEAD NOT ONLY WITH VISION BUT ALSO WITH OUR VALUES.

Chapter 2

Determine Your Values

I married a man who was blessed with a long career as a defenseman in the National Hockey League. It's a good thing that titles don't impress me much, since he retired from the game nearly a decade ago.

What impressed me about Keith when I met him back in 1995 wasn't what he did on the ice, but what he did while walking through the lower level of the arena to the parking lot after games. Regardless of whether his team had won or lost the game, I consistently witnessed Keith greet every worker, every intern, every custodian, every parking attendant, every single person he came in contact with—regardless of status—with kindness, humility, respect, and gratitude.

I fell in love with my husband not for what he did, but for who he was and continues to be. It's no surprise that, twenty years later, this is the same person who was able to say yes to adopting another man's child and caring for him as he does his own. Who Keith appeared to be when we were first dating is the same person who continues to show up in my life now, because a strong character doesn't fade away when a job title does.

As parents, let's not focus on raising people who may hold prestigious titles one day. Instead, let's concentrate our efforts on building up men and women with strong value systems. I am forever grateful to my in-laws for the man of character that they raised, and I would love for my son- and daughters-in-law to be able to say the same thing of their spouses one day.

A strong character is sustaining. A strong resume is not. Therefore, we must raise children focused on WHO they are and not WHAT they do.

When we visualize our child graduating from high school, we must be careful not to make college or career the main ambition. Because when this becomes the end goal, our parental focus becomes fixed on getting our child into the right school, into the right classes, and with the right teachers. And then, we make sure they get the right grades and sign up for the right extracurricular activities and community service opportunities. All of this strategizing is done to try to ensure that the right resume is built, which will hopefully get them into the right college which will then land them their dream job.

AS PARENTS, OUR "JOB" IS TO PURPOSELY INSTILL A SOLID VALUE SYSTEM IN OUR CHILDREN SO THAT THEIR LIVES BRING VALUE TO OTHERS AND THE WORLD AROUND THEM.

God doesn't care about GPAs or SAT scores, so we needn't be so hung up on them either. He doesn't care what college our kids end up going to or what job they will have afterward. He cares about their heart and soul, and how they choose to treat others with the resources that He has given them.

As parents, our "job" is to purposely instill a solid value system in our children so that their lives bring value to others and the world around them.

WHAT'S THE PROBLEM?

Purposely transferring our values to our children is one of the most important things we need to do as a parent. If we don't pass our values on to our kids, someone else will.

The problem is that today's culture is so distracted by status and success that many parents mistakenly make these the goal of parenthood. In past generations, parents strived to raise good citizens and neighbors. Today, it seems we are more worried about our kids possessing a strong resume than a strong value system. If that's true, it's time we made a purposeful shift.

The Mixed Messages We Send

In today's world, our youth's values appear to be awry, and the messages that we're sending as adults—even if unintentionally—may be at the heart of the problem.

When our child gets straight A's on a report card, we feel like a successful parent and proudly beam before rewarding our son or daughter with monetary compensation or a celebratory dinner. When they score a goal or win the game, we cheer loudly and proudly from the sidelines.

We celebrate the good grades, the victories, the accolades, the performances, and the achievements because the results are easily measured. It's natural to be proud of our offspring when they are visibly succeeding in their academics and activities, making us believe that we are doing something right as a parent to have such successful children. But what happens when that child helps a sibling with homework or assists a neighbor out of the kindness of their heart, is there any fanfare or praise?

Is it possible, that amidst the striving for success, we are forgetting to develop timeless values and lasting character traits in our children?

Good Grades or Good People?

If I asked you whether it was more important that your child achieve good grades or be a good person, I know what you would say. If you are taking the time to read a parenting book, I assume your goal is to raise a good person over a good student, right? We know that's what is important overall, yet I'm not so sure that this is the message that our children are actually receiving from us.

In the 2017 *Highlights* "The State of the Kid" report, students ages six to twelve were asked what was most important to their parents: that they are kind, happy, or that they do well in school.[i] Unfortunately, among these three values, kindness ranked last.

We saw a similar gap in Harvard's Making Caring Common Project 2014 report, "The Children We Mean to Raise." While research indicates that 96% of parents report that moral character in children is "very important, if not essential," 81% of the kids surveyed said that happiness or achievement is their parents' top priority.[ii]

The interviewees were also three times more likely to agree that, "My parents are prouder if I get good grades in my classes than if I'm a caring community member in class and school." I have a hard time believing that this is what parents genuinely want, yet this truth is our youth's perspective.

As parents, we say compassion and empathy are traits that we want our child to embody, yet serving others is the last thing we schedule on our overpacked calendar. Therefore, our sons and daughters learn that we fit in helping others *after* serving ourselves. We will talk more about how to change this in chapter nine.

Maybe gratitude is another value you deem essential, yet do you expect your children to take the time to write handwritten thank you notes for the gifts they receive? Or, do you allow them to receive without acknowledgment?

If we want our children to learn pertinent values, then we have to take the time to teach them.

Perhaps a strong work ethic is important, yet you continue to do everything for your child because you feel badly asking them to get a job or to do chores since they are so busy with their schoolwork and activities. However, contributing to the family is the way the value of hard work is first developed.

What about respect? We want to raise respectful children, yet we sometimes model disrespect to their teachers, coaches, or employers by questioning their leadership.

We may say faith is our number one value, yet we sit on the sidelines of our kids' sports competitions instead of next to one another in a church pew.

WHAT'S THE SOLUTION?

Mind the Value Gap

There is a gap between what parents say are their top priorities and the real messages they convey in their behavior day to day. Because we have such a powerful influence on children's values, it's no small matter when there is a gap between what we say and what we appear to prioritize daily.

When parents' daily messages about achievement and happiness drown out their messages about concern for others, children tend not to prioritize caring and fairness. They're more likely to be preoccupied with their own needs rather than the needs of others, and entitlement and selfish behaviors are often the result.

In order to close the gap between what we say we value and the messages that our kids are internalizing, we must focus on WHO we want our child to be, rather than WHAT we want them to become. We must confidently lead our child to opportunities and experiences where they can authentically absorb the values we want them to have.

Build a Value Village

There is so much truth to the African proverb, "It takes a village to raise a child." It takes a community of different people interacting with a child in order for them to learn the values we want them to know. Be proactive in purposely surrounding your family with a community that aligns with your vision and values. Your child's basketball coach or English teacher may authentically hold the same views or values as you, but they may not. To build your value village, you may need to look beyond your child's daily mentors at school or in their activities.

Get more involved in your place of worship and let your children learn from the leaders and community there. Begin looking for non-profit organizations where your family can regularly serve and build relationships with others who share your values.

If I want my children to grow strong in their faith, I need to give them opportunities to learn from men and women who are living out their faith in action. It's why Keith and I take our kids on regular medical mission trips with their dentist to the Yucatan instead of taking vacations to see Mickey and Minnie at the Happiest Place on Earth. It's also one of the main reasons we send our children to be mentored by faith-filled young adults at Kanakuk sleepaway summer camp in Missouri, instead of enrolling them in private school.

In order for us to make the best choices while raising our children, we must first clarify what core values we purposely want to hand down.

STRATEGIES TO CONSIDER

A parent is a child's first teacher and role model. Value education begins with you, which means it is your responsibility to teach your child what you want them to know. The beloved and longtime host of *Mister Rogers' Neighborhood* Fred Rogers said, "You rarely have time for everything you want in this life, so you need to make choices. And hopefully your choices can come from a deep sense of who you are."[iii]

> **"YOU RARELY HAVE TIME FOR EVERYTHING YOU WANT IN THIS LIFE, SO YOU NEED TO MAKE CHOICES. AND HOPEFULLY YOUR CHOICES CAN COME FROM A DEEP SENSE OF WHO YOU ARE."**
> — **FRED ROGERS**

Claim Your Core Values

In order for us to make the best choices for our children, we must first clarify what core values we purposely want to hand down. One day, I asked my Facebook followers to list the values they thought we were failing to teach children today. The responses were many: respect, gratitude, humility, honesty, compassion, empathy, hard work, and the list went on. It proved that values do matter to us.

What values matter to you?

Begin by looking at your spouse or your best friend and jot down the endearing traits and virtues they possess. You can always count on the Bible, like I do, to lead you as well.

I'm so grateful I don't have to wonder what to focus on instilling in my children as I can start with what the Bible tells us in Galatians 5:22-23. These nine fruits of the Spirit are essential core values for life and leadership: love, joy, peace, patience, kindness, goodness, faithfulness, gentleness, and self-control.

Be the Example

We must be the adults we want our children to grow up to be. To become a productive and successful leader for our children, we must first intentionally live out our values in our own lives. "Who we are and how we engage with the world is a far more accurate predictor of how our children will do than what we know about parenting," says Brené Brown, author and research professor at the University of Houston Graduate College of Social Work.[iv]

Our kids are constantly watching to see if our actions (what we do and say) match the expectations that we set for them. What do your kids see you value? What do they witness you post on social media? How do they watch you spend your money and your time?

If I say faith is the cornerstone of my life, yet my children see me worship God only when there's open availability on our busy calendar, what does this show my sons and daughter? It shows them that you can say something is a priority without having to make it one.

If my children see me only helping other people when it's convenient or comfortable for me, they will grow up understanding that they should always look out for themselves first. **What our kids watch us do, not what they hear us say, is what they will know to be true about life.** What our children see with their eyes is more important than what they will hear with their ears. Our children will follow our example and not our advice.

GET STARTED TODAY!

Remember that a strong character is sustaining. A strong resume is not. Therefore, we must raise children into adults focused on WHO they are and not WHAT they do. The good thing is no matter where you find yourself amidst your season of full-time parenthood, your family screenplay is still being written. You have time to pause, pivot, and plan for changes that you want and need to make.

Pause

What is your present reality?

As a leader of your family, take the time to determine your core family values. What are you striving to instill in your child that will sustain them as an adult?

Pivot

What do you want to keep the same? What do you want to do differently?

Look at your calendar and see where you are spending the majority of your time, money, and energy. Is there a gap in what you say is your priority, and what you are currently prioritizing?

Plan

What action can you take to move things in the direction you want to go?

Purposely work to close your value gap. List ways to authentically teach the values you want to instill in your child. Need inspiration to help clarify your family values?

Go to Appendix B for a list of 92 Values and Virtues. Highlight the ones that stand out to you and begin to focus on instilling those.

 NEXT UP: PARENTS, WE MUST PURPOSELY LEAD NOT ONLY WITH VISION, AND VALUES, BUT WITH AUTHORITY.

Chapter 3

Claim Your Authority

The monotony of my daily routine tending to my newborn triplets was interrupted by the trill of the doorbell. The chime caught me off guard as our family was new to the Orange County neighborhood, and I wasn't expecting anyone.

I opened the door to a friendly neighbor who introduced herself as Maureen. As she handed me a basket of goodies welcoming us to the neighborhood, she asked, "Have you put your sons on the St. Paul Preschool waiting list yet?"

Strangers constantly asked us questions—if triplets ran in our family, if I was breastfeeding them, etc.—but no one had yet inquired about the plans Keith and I had to educate our trio. It was apparent my new neighbor friend was not in touch with my current reality.

"You will never get them into that preschool if you don't go put them on the waiting list now," continued Maureen.

Preschool? Waiting list? Now? What in the world was this woman talking about?

Could she not see that this momma on the other side of the threshold was barely making it through each day? One look at my disheveled appearance should have clued her in to the fact that the boys' path to Harvard hadn't yet crossed my mind. Our sons would go off to school one day, but why was she bringing it up now, when their education was irrelevant?

In the three months since I'd given birth in Arizona and moved to California, I hadn't thought past anything more than my longing for a good night's sleep.

I still lingered on the crucial choices between Huggies or Pampers? Enfamil or Similac? Cry it out or get the pacifier?

The moment I shut the door behind my neighbor, I realized that my husband and I might need to begin thinking more about the future of our family, even though we were bogged down with parenting in the present.

I needed to move beyond the routine tasks that consumed my days, whether I felt prepared to do that or not. I realized my parenting purpose wasn't just to take care of my sons, but to lead them into their future. Yikes! Now that was an overwhelming truth I wanted to ignore because I soon realized this is much easier said than done.

WHAT'S THE PROBLEM?

When our kids were in that perfect little preschool (thanks to Maureen's advice), I began reading articles about how parents were failing to lead this generation of children. College students were entering campuses prepared on paper, but profoundly unprepared for real life. Twenty-year-olds were still overly dependent on their parents and possessed few coping or problem-solving skills. Employers and coaches had to coddle entitled young adults who thought the world revolved around them because no one had told them otherwise.

As a parent of four little kids, I wanted to understand how young adults could arrive at college ill prepared for real life. And, was there anything I could do to prevent this from happening to my own children?

What did I need to do as a parent to raise my children into strong adults who would be valuable to the world around them?

Keith and I know we want to raise capable, confident, and compassionate adults. I want to launch my children with a smile on my face, just as my mom did me. I also want to get together with other parents and talk about more exciting things than what's going on with our twelve-year old's soccer team.

Why is this so difficult today?

The problem is, unlike past generations, American parents are no longer functioning as strong family leaders. But why?

It's likely because many parents have decided that good parenting now means doing everything for your child, to try to ensure their happiness and success. Besides nurturing, loving, and teaching our children, we have added other roles to our job description.

> **As a parent, our "job" is to be a strong leader and authority figure who can confidently guide our child into adulthood.**

We are now a handyman, who fixes everything that breaks. We are a landscaper, who mows down everyone and everything that happens to get in the way of developing our perfectly manicured child. We have become cruise directors, who tirelessly plan a blissful childhood itinerary of entertainment, amusement, and happiness. We've taken on the role of air traffic controller, directing everyone toward the proper path to success. And most detrimental of all, we've become a BFF to our child, who really needs a parent leader instead.

Why have we added all of these mistaken identities to our role as parent? Because culture has us overwhelmed, distracted, and confused about the true purpose of parenting. We've given authorship of our family stories to popular culture and—often unintentionally—have checked out of our leadership role, becoming a pal instead of a parent.

As explained by author and psychologist, John Rosemond, who also wrote the foreword to this book, "Leadership is weakened by the well-intentioned attempt to be 'popular' with one's children. The truly loving parent is one who provides not just ample nurturing, but effective discipline and effective leadership."[v]

As a parent, our "job" is to be a strong leader and authority figure who can confidently guide our child into adulthood.

WHAT'S THE SOLUTION?

Let's back up to the beginning of time and see what the Bible tells us our purpose is as a parent. Proverbs 22:6 says, "Train up a child in the way he should go; even when he is old, he will not depart from it." Whether you are a person of faith or not, this timeless verse plainly states our parental purpose—to train, teach, lead, mentor, and guide the children in our care, whether they are toddlers or teenagers.

Be Proactive Not Reactive

After birthing four kids within eighteen months, it is an understatement to say that I merely survived motherhood for many years. My only goal was to keep everyone alive and asleep for as long as possible. I spent each day reacting to whatever came my way. I raised my children like I was playing an old school game of Whac-a-Mole. I hovered over the game of parenthood, waiting for a mole to rear its little head so I could whack at it until it would retreat into its hole. Got it. Whack. Next dilemma. Whack. Many of us continue to reactively raise our child like this until they move into adulthood, and then we question whether we should have taken a better approach.

The parenting purpose statement that you learned about in the first chapter will help you to be proactive when making decisions.

We don't need to wait for our ten-year-old to beg for a cell phone and then reactively run out and buy an iPhone for her birthday because she said she wanted it. Begin to decide now when might be a good age to own a first cell phone in your family. Do your research, and don't be afraid to do things differently than your neighbor.

Don't wait until your son is headed off to kindergarten to figure out what type of education you want him to have. Begin to look at the options in your area now. If the public school around the corner from you is not a good fit, then begin to search for one that aligns with your vision, values, and the overall goals you named in your parenting purpose statement.

Don't wait until your child turns sixteen to begin thinking about a driver's license, a part-time job, or dating. Begin thinking now about what it will look like to be a teenager in your family. How will you define responsibilities, freedoms, and boundaries for your child?

We must look ahead to the future and then confidently lead our children accordingly. If, when our child is young, we determine an appropriate age for them to do or own certain things, then we won't be easily persuaded by peer pressure or cajoling from our child before that time.

Make Conscious Decisions

When I was pregnant with our triplets, Keith and I purposely purchased a house across the street from one of the area's top public elementary schools so that we would never have to find ourselves in a drop-off or pickup line—ever. Years later, when our kids walked themselves across the street, we considered ourselves to be brilliant parents until we witnessed our neighbors racing their uniformed students out of the neighborhood to charter and private schools, leaving us questioning if we were doing right by our children.

Isn't this precisely what we struggle with today? We question the decisions we make in our family when we see other parents doing things differently.

We look at the friend who sends her children off to a specialized summer camp and wonder if we should sign our kids up too.

We receive an invitation for our daughter to join a prestigious organization, and since we'd hate for her to miss out on such a great opportunity, we sign her up without even thinking if this meets the end goal we have for her.

We watch our boss take his family on a mission trip to Guatemala, so we begin to question if our kids need to do this as well.

We are better able to lead our children with confidence when we take the time and make the effort to claim our family vision, values, and purpose.

STRATEGIES TO CONSIDER

Decide to be the CEO of Your Home

Think of your family and your home as a company in which you and your partner are the CEOs. In this scenario, your focus becomes being an active leader—neither a pushover nor a dictator. In every situation, you remember that you are the leader, capable and confident as you provide guidance, training, and encouragement.

Running a successful organization and running a healthy family are very similar. Great parents use the same leadership skills within the family that effective managers use in the workplace. If you review current trends in business leadership and management strategies, it's clear that many of them are highly relevant to creating healthy families and raising resilient children.

In fact, it is why many authors turn their leadership books into titles specifically geared towards parents. Leadership guru, Stephen R. Covey, took his *7 Habits of Highly Effective People* and released a version for parents called *7 Habits of Highly Effective Families*. More recently, author Amy Morin took her book *13 Things Mentally Strong People Don't Do* and turned it into *13 Things Mentally Strong Parents Don't Do*.

So, take your favorite business leadership book and apply the principles to raising your child. Like it or not, leadership has to start with you, the parent. Raising a child well will take a lot of effort and hard work. The world needs us to be up for the challenge.

Strengthen Your Leadership Skills

Look over the following list of qualities commonly attributed to great leaders.

A LEADER …

- has an authoritative presence.
- communicates expectations.
- claims goals for the group.
- makes courageous and sometimes unpopular choices.
- knows he must create boundaries between himself and his followers.
- possesses integrity.
- walks their talk.

Choose one leadership quality from the list above and begin strengthening that area in yourself. As you develop that skill, you'll start to gain confidence and establish a foundation from which you can make the decisions that you know will meet your family goals. For example, don't ask your child if they want to get their driver's license when they turn sixteen, tell them in advance that, in your family, it's what they will be doing.

GET STARTED TODAY!

It's never too late to brush up on your leadership skills. Take some time to pause, pivot, and plan for the changes that you want and need to make as a leader in your family.

Pause

What is your present reality?

Look at the parents you admire. Think about why their styles resonate with you, and examine how they behave, manage, and motivate their kids to see if those styles hold clues you can use to improve your own leadership skills and approach.

Pivot

What do you want to keep the same? What do you want to do differently?

If you need to bring more authority to your parental role, plan a family meeting and discuss how and why you are going to change a few things in your newfound role as CEO. Share the importance of your family vision, values, and purpose with your children.

Plan

What action can you take to move things in the direction you want to go?

As a family leader, maybe you need to take the time to spell out clear expectations, boundaries, and consequences for your children. Take the time to figure out what is currently not working in your family and make the effort to address it.

NEXT UP: PARENTS, WE MUST PURPOSELY STRENGTHEN OUR FAMILY IDENTITY, CULTURE, AND RELATIONSHIPS.

PART 2:
LOVE

love on purpose

THE FAMILY THAT **PLAYS TOGETHER** *STAYS TOGETHER* 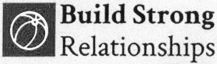 **Build Strong** Relationships

develop your unique family culture

Be playful. Be *silly.* **Have more** *fun.*

 LAUGH MORE *PLAY MORE* CONNECT MORE

Prioritize Team Family Put Down the Screens *Go Outside and Play*

slow down *RELAX* *live* life

MAKE SPACE FOR CREATIVITY, CURIOSITY AND IMAGINATION

936 weeks *from Birth to 18*

Celebrate simple moments

Make the time. Make the effort. **Create lasting memories.**

 Timeless *Traditions*

SEEK Solitude

GATHER TOGETHER. TALK OFTEN. **DISCONNECT TO RECONNECT**

Cultivate sacred family spaces

This is us. *This is who we are.* THIS IS WHAT WE DO

 Strong Families *Spend Time* Together Often

 Replace Mindless *Screen Time With* Meaningful Family Time

device-free DINNERS

www.amycarney.com

Chapter 4

Prioritize Play

We had been on the road nearly two and a half months, traveling the country in our motorhome, before I fully grasped why we had chosen to play hooky from our regularly scheduled programming back at home in Arizona. We were overnighting in Nowhere, Indiana, when I figured it out.

Our family of six ended up on this adventure because we had to stop the madness that was our daily life. Before we pulled the plug on our normal existence, our days were constantly spent apart from one another. Keith drove one direction, and I drove another as we continuously sat—separately—on the sidelines of our kids' lives, cheering them on at their competitions and school activities. We knew we needed to regain control of our family story. We wanted to enjoy this season of raising our four preteens, so an epic experience like this seemed like the medicine our disconnected family needed. But I hadn't realized precisely what was lacking in our lives until the fireflies reminded me.

As the night sky fell upon us, our kids were in awe of the scores of flickering yellow lights surrounding them. In an instant, the simplicity of my carefree childhood came rushing back. Catching lightning bugs was a rite of passage for a child growing up just three hours north of where we were camping in Evansville. I grabbed plastic cups from our tiny cupboard and made tops out of tin foil, so we could go … play … together … outside.

While I had spent my childhood chasing fireflies, my children were growing up chasing after A's in the classroom or the next W on the sports field. Before we took off in an RV for a seven-month tour of the USA, our family had little space for relaxed outdoor play. Organized sports, screens, schooling, and scheduled activities consumed childhood's narrative for the people growing up in our care.

On a night when Keith and I would have been shuttling kids around to their various endeavors, we were, instead, playing outside together—laughing and breathing in the beauty of catching fireflies and simply being a family. The fireflies reminded me that our family needed to create more space for happy, playful moments like this, even after we returned home from our grand tour.

In between the hustle and bustle of daily life, it's the playful moments, big and small, that strengthen our relationships. Strong families spend time together often. Spending time with your child, no matter their age, sends a simple message—you matter and my relationship with you is important.

WHAT'S THE PROBLEM?

"Go outside and play," which was once a universal phrase used by American parents, has now been replaced with: "Get in the car we have to go!"; "Get off the screens!"; "Is your homework done?"; and "Hurry up."

The problem is we rush our kids through their childhood without insisting they find time to simply go out and play.

Instead of seeing kids leisurely playing together after school and on the weekends, we see minivans and SUVs rushing children out of the neighborhood and off to the next competition or lesson. Even if the child isn't performing that day, we still don't see them because they are inside in front of a screen—making the sofa or desk chair their preferred place "to play." I wish I could tell you that I couldn't relate, but unfortunately our home is no exception to the modern scenario.

This new American childhood that adults have created is taking its toll on the well-being and happiness of our children. According to Darell Hammond, founder of KaBOOM: "Play is essential to the proper development, socialization, and physical, emotional, and mental health of children. Without ample time for play, all of these areas are negatively impacted."[vi]

Before our RV family sabbatical in 2014, Keith and I thought our children were playing a lot. If they weren't in school, they were "playing" a sport. But, I'm not sure that youth sports today can be classified as the positive play our children need in their lives. There's a big difference between how my children felt running around catching fireflies and how they feel catching ground balls night after night with a coach telling them what move to make next.

Youth Sports Cost Us

Soccer sounded like a healthy activity for our daughter when we signed her up at the age of six. However, what began as a carefree endeavor where she could get exercise and make friends, quickly became a consuming family commitment. On weeknights, we were required to shuttle her back and forth to nightly practices. On weekends, our time was spent on the sidelines of games, tournaments, and competitions. And then, somehow, we got to the point of driving or flying out of state and overnighting in hotels on holiday weekends—all because our athletic daughter wanted to have fun playing a sport with friends.

Now, soccer is a part of her identity. It keeps our daughter off technology and in good physical condition, plus her teammates are her friends. Therefore, we allow her to continue in competitive soccer, but it comes at a cost—not only to our bank account but to our overall family narrative as well.

Sometimes, our individual and family playtime is diminished because of one child's commitment. It becomes difficult to squeeze in dinners around the family table when our kids are involved in these consuming activities. We may also be left with little time or money for family vacations or special outings because the calendar is filled with performances, lessons, and camps requiring their participation and our funds.

And, if we're honest, we're not sure if we can consider any of this fun. Yet, this is our sons' and daughter's version of childhood "playtime" today, while sitting on the sidelines cheering them on has, sadly enough, become ours.

AS PARENTS, OUR "JOB" IS TO STEP AWAY FROM THE ORGANIZED ACTIVITIES AND MORE FREQUENTLY CREATE ROOM FOR AUTHENTIC LIFE GIVING MOMENTS OF PLAY FOR OUR CHILDREN AND OURSELVES.

I wish I could tell you that we came home from the RV trip and boldly had our kids quit all of their competitive organized activities. I may have been all for that, but our teens love their sports, and there are wonderful aspects to being part of a team. So, we have allowed our sons and daughter to continue to this day. But what Keith and I fully understand now is that we must carve out space in our performance-driven culture to prioritize Team Family now and again. We must slow down and enjoy doing something that fuels our souls instead of the resumes.

As parents, our "job" is to step away from the organized activities and more frequently create room for authentic life giving moments of play for our children and ourselves.

Consequences of Play Deprivation

"The opposite of play is not work—the opposite of play is depression," said play theorist Brian Sutton-Smith.[vii] What happens if we don't take the time to play? Could our country's high suicide rates of today be linked to play deprivation in our lives? What if incorporating more play into our lives is the key to lowering anxiety, depression, addictive disorders, and obesity?

Psychiatrist and founder of the National Institute of Play, Stuart Brown, MD, originally coined the term "play deprivation" in 2001, and he claims that play deprivation is now an acute public health crisis. "Mother Nature embedded Play as a fundamental survival drive, into us, and like sleep, when we don't play, negative compensations emerge over time, and our lives become dull and joyless."[viii]

Peter Gray, PhD, a research professor at Boston College says, "When parents realize the major role that free play can take in the development of emotionally healthy children and adults, they may wish to reassess the priorities ruling their children's lives." He adds that, "Without ample play, we will continue to see a decrease in creativity and imagination, as well as vital skills like problem-solving, social skills, the ability to assess risk and resiliency. All of these not only help prepare children to learn more effectively in school but help prepare them for successful adulthood."[ix]

Brown, in his book, *Play*, goes further to claim that play is essential for adults, as well as children, in fueling happiness and intelligence throughout our lives. He believes that the importance of play isn't just for kids; it is imperative throughout our lifetime.

It's time we, as parents, reduce the scheduled, organized activities; limit or get rid of video games, televisions, and handheld devices; and demand our children "go outside and play" again.

WHAT'S THE SOLUTION?

Play is the secret ingredient to successful families. If you want a happy family, play more. Focusing more on silliness in our homes instead of SAT scores may catapult our children further in life and strengthen our families overall.

Isn't successful adulthood what we said we are aiming for when raising our child? Then play we must! Playtime cannot be optional; we must view it as a mandatory part of a healthy life.

Life's primary pursuit certainly shouldn't be pleasure or amusement, but parents must realize the significant role that free play (a.k.a. fun) can make in the development of emotionally healthy children and adults.

Make Playtime Mandatory

"Play is the joy of being fully present and engaged in a process, without fear or failure—a pleasant venture into the unknown," said Arizona play advocate, Dana Keller. "When we are present and engaged in play activities, we are saying that we are not committed to an end result. Play is a break from the ordinary that provides fun, creativity, learning, spontaneity, and collaboration/connection."[x]

"WHEN WE ARE PRESENT AND ENGAGED IN PLAY ACTIVITIES, WE ARE SAYING THAT WE ARE NOT COMMITTED TO AN END RESULT. PLAY IS A BREAK FROM THE ORDINARY THAT PROVIDES FUN, CREATIVITY, LEARNING, SPONTANEITY, AND CONNECTION."
– DANA KELLER

Maybe you're like me and don't love playing sports or sitting on the floor for a game of Candyland. Maybe you think that play is a useless waste of time, and it's not for you. I felt the same way until I better understood the benefits play offered. It's the feeling we got seeing those fireflies.

It's felt in those spontaneous, carefree moments that we seize in the middle of an ordinary day, and in the hobbies and pastimes that provide us with a break from the monotony of our routines. It's the feeling I get when I hike the mountains in Arizona and in those moments when the kids teach me the latest dance moves and then laugh at me when I attempt them. It's dropping my daughter off at the soccer field and then going to the Bible journaling class that I want to attend. It's going to the farmers market with my husband. Play is doing things that get you out of the daily grind and bring your soul joy.

Cultivate a Playful Home

Our homes must be a place where play is not only welcomed but encouraged. The key is to regularly weave small playful moments into your family culture.

I wouldn't consider our family members to be naturally silly people out in the real world. We are fairly reserved introverts, yet we have no problem being silly and laughing together in our home. We sing even though no one is a singer. We dance even though no one is a dancer. We do yoga poses together although I am the only practicing yogi. We own karaoke machines, a turntable with records, and musical instruments. We have closets full of games, puzzles, books, and art supplies.

We must do what it takes to relax, slow down, and create space in our existence for family fun. For us, that meant a total family reboot in a motorhome—away from everything that distracted us on a daily basis—so that we could catch some fireflies.

STRATEGIES TO CONSIDER

How can we restore play in our lives?

Put Away the Screens

In our downtime, adults and kids alike can easily get absorbed by technology or television if we're not mindful. We must be conscious not to let our sons' playtime consist of wearing headphones and holding a game controller in their hands. Constantly playing video games is not a healthy, life-giving form of play. Nor is allowing our daughter to sit behind a closed door, binge-watching Netflix or YouTube videos in her spare time.

Remember, a "go outside and play" (rather than a "sit inside and stare") mentality will better develop the type of adult we want to launch into the world. We must be brave parents and limit the screens. (More tips on this coming up in the next chapter!)

Reduce Structured Activities

Kids need time to be kids—to play, make friends, relax, and have fun. Putting children in too many adult-led programs robs them of the opportunity to make their own fun and play by their own rules. Today, we see many children waiting for adult instruction before they enter into a playful activity. We must allow our children more space and free time, so they can instead learn how to develop initiative. Create space for more self-directed play and fewer organized activities.

Invest in Playful Experiences

Invest your money and time into experiences that will connect your family through play. Go to your local toy store and buy a new board game or puzzle. Perhaps purchase bicycles so you can ride around your community searching for geocaches or letterboxes—both of which we did a lot of while on our family tour of the US.

Consider investing in sleepaway summer camp for your kids. This is one of the ways Keith and I invest in community play for our teenagers for a few weeks each summer. We invest in the opportunity for them to go to Kanakuk summer camp in the Ozarks to spend time in God's country, without technology or parents telling them what move to make next.

It's also important to model an interesting, playful life for your kids. Do your kids see you go off and do what you love to do? Do they see you meet up to do fun things with friends? Don't simply follow your loved ones around and constantly watch them "play." We adults must carve out playtime in our lives, too.

GET STARTED TODAY!

As parents, one of the most important things we can do is regularly evaluate our family priorities to determine whether we are truly living life in accordance with what we say and believe to be important. Is there a gap between what you desire and your current reality?

Pause

What is your present reality?

Stop and compare memories of your childhood playtime to your children's current schedules. What is different? Do you and your child have space for boredom, creativity, curiosity and imagination in your lives? How might you be restricting your child's outdoor play?

Pivot

What do you want to keep the same? What do you want to do differently?

How would your kids say you play together in your family? In order to make play a priority in your family, you must purposely prioritize it. Make a list of your personal and family "playgrounds" and then schedule time on your calendar to get to them. "Playgrounds" are simply places where you go to have fun, such as the bowling alley or to one of our family favorites-an Escape the Room venue.

Plan

What action can you take to move things in the direction you want to go?

Give the gift of play. For birthday and holiday gift giving, don't buy your children electronics for presents, even though that may be what they say they want. Instead, purposely invest in things that can bring playful moments to your family. Invest in something that will get your kids playing outdoors together. What can you get that will encourage your family members to gather around the table together? Don't buy products that will further disconnect your family. Instead seek out products that will strengthen sibling and family relationships.

Go to www.AmyCarney.com to check out our family's playtime favorites and to access my Parent on Purpose Amazon store.

NEXT UP: PARENTS, WE MUST PURPOSELY PUT THE DEVICES DOWN AND BUILD STRONG RELATIONSHIP WITH ONE ANOTHER FACE-TO-FACE.

Chapter 5

Disconnect to Reconnect

Sitting in church one Sunday, I watched an older couple in front of me continuously scroll Facebook while our pastor preached an engaging sermon. Off to my right, a preteen girl was oblivious to her surroundings as she sat next to her mother playing video games on her device. Another woman held her phone at shoulder level as she recorded a video of the entire service. None of them were aware that their digital distractions were distracting not only them, but all of us around them.

Why is it that people can't even worship now without a device in their hand?

Look around any restaurant or public gathering spot today. It's the rare group of people who are engaged in conversation with one another instead of consumed with a technological device. Everywhere I go, I see toddlers captivated by iPads and teenage girls posing together for selfies to post. And now, adults in their sixties can't even sit through a church service without constantly turning to a screen to entertain them. What in the world is going on? Why are we, adults and children, so obsessed with our digital devices?

We are allowing technology to change us. We've already established that playtime has been replaced with screen time. But, our vision, values, and purpose are also being compromised as we spend more time connecting to Wi-Fi than we do connecting in person with our family and friends.

We are allowing technology to change childhood, too. It's not a child's fault that he no longer wants to play with Legos, create works of art, or hang out with family members in his downtime. Who wants to put forth the effort when you can be endlessly entertained by easier and more exciting things on screens instead?

Who wants to go outside and play with unfamiliar kids in the neighborhood when you can comfortably sit inside and connect with your "real" friends online?

Playing outdoors, spending time with friends, reading books, and hanging out with family is happening a lot less because we are allowing our kids to spend their free time Minecrafting, Instagramming, YouTubing, and Netflixing. And, all of this screen time is creating disconnection in our relationships and our lives.

Let's look back at the first section of this book and what we said our vision, values, and purpose were. I highly doubt video games, social media, or surfing the internet had any part in your parenting purpose statement, yet so often we allow screens to overtake our daily narratives.

What is it that you said you value? If we say we value hard work, then how can we allow our sons or daughters to sit inside for hours on end with a technological device in hand, virtually communicating with strangers online instead of expecting them to help around the house or in the community?

We say our family relationships are our priority, yet we allow our children to put on headphones and ignore us in the car or sit behind a closed door shooting animated figures on a screen or mindlessly scroll social media channels instead of communicating face-to-face with us.

We say humility is something we value, yet we post every enjoyable aspect of our lives online for all to see.

We say compassion and empathy are essential, yet we don't take the time to put down the devices and get to know people and what's going on in their lives.

Parents, we must be aware of what we are allowing technology to do to us and our children and purposely begin to make bold changes.

WHAT'S THE PROBLEM?

Technology might be the most significant battlefield we are facing as parents when raising children in popular culture today. However, technology is not the problem—our time and habits on our screens are the issue.

As digital rookies, many parents are unsure how to best lead their children in this overwhelming new space. We know too much screen time isn't healthy, yet we're not quite sure what to do. And while we try to figure it out, our child's brain, relationships, and values slowly succumb to the pitfalls of technology.

The problem is we don't always think through the ramifications of giving our child technology. They want it. We believe they need it; so, we get it. It's what the world around us seems to do, so we follow suit and then find ourselves scrambling to control it. If we are willing to give children access to these devices, then we must be willing to put forth the effort it takes to train our son or daughter how to balance screen life with real life.

I've often found myself dreaming about living on Amish farmland, free of all this technological madness. Unfortunately, we're not Amish and never will be, so I must face the reality of living with technology as a major part of our existence. Keith and I must figure out how to help our children best manage their screens so that the devices are a blessing to our lives instead of a curse.

The worst thing we can do is hand over access to the internet and let our kids begin to hide behind headphones and closed doors. Sure, we may lovingly give our child an iDevice to be in close connection to us and their friends, but I hope you realize how easily this also can connect them to pornography and pedophiles who lurk online. Parents, we must pay attention and be diligently involved.

> AS PARENTS, OUR "JOB" IS TO HELP OUR CHILDREN LEARN SMART DIGITAL CITIZENSHIP AND SELF-REGULATION WHILE UNDER OUR GUIDANCE.

As parents, our "job" is to help our children learn smart digital citizenship and self-regulation while under our guidance.

WHAT'S THE SOLUTION?

We must purposely create screen-free environments that support conversation and face-to-face communication.

Designate Screen-Free Spaces

Time around the family table is sacred space; therefore, we need to make all mealtimes screen free. This is where you will hear the stories, the struggles, the joys, and the sorrows.

Family mealtime connections will strengthen the heart of your family if you forbid the presence of screens during that time. Put away the devices and engage with the people you get to enjoy a meal with. It doesn't matter if you're at the family dining table or out at a restaurant together, don't allow devices to distract you from building authentic relationships with one another.

Besides mealtimes, protect your child's sleep time as well by keeping digital devices and televisions out of bedrooms. Designate a family charging station in the central area of your home where devices live overnight. Buy old-school alarm clocks to wake your children in the morning. Also, expect all screen time to occur in open family areas.

Encourage Solitude

All of us need time to be alone with ourselves so that we can figure out exactly who we are without a device to distract us. "Always connected, we see loneliness as a problem that technology should solve. The necessary conversations of solitude and self-reflection are endangered," says Sherry Turkle, author of *Reclaiming Conversation*. "Reclaiming conversation begins with reclaiming our capacity for solitude."[xi] She continues in the book to say that children can't develop the capacity for solitude if they don't have the experience of being "bored" and then turning within, rather than to a screen.

Knowing that developing the capacity for solitude is an important task of childhood, Keith and I want to make sure our family has plenty of screen-free space to reflect and renew our minds and souls. This means our kids must witness us, as adults, eating meals alone or simply hanging out at home without a device in our hands or a screen in front of us. All adults, and children alike, must fight the impulse to turn to our devices for constant company and comfort.

Incorporating a ritual of screen-free Sundays or tech-free Tuesdays into your family culture is a great way to purposely create margin for boredom, creativity, and playful moments. Designate a particular day or regular timeframe where your family intentionally turns off the devices as a way to show that you are in control of technology instead of it controlling you.

Construct Supportive Social Environments

We need to give our children space to create meaningful memories that are not connected to a screen. "The goal is to help your children develop a level of competency that will allow them opportunities to succeed and learn how to find balance for an active, healthy lifestyle," says Dr. Lisa Strohman, founder and director of Digital Citizen Academy.[xii]

> "ALWAYS CONNECTED, WE SEE LONELINESS AS A PROBLEM THAT TECHNOLOGY SHOULD SOLVE. THE NECESSARY CONVERSATIONS OF SOLITUDE AND SELF-REFLECTION ARE ENDANGERED."
> – SHERRY TURKLE

How will our children ever learn who they truly are and develop the interpersonal skills they need if we don't give them opportunities to free themselves from the pressures of social media and the internet? Like I've already mentioned, Keith and I purposely send our kids off to technology-free sleepaway summer camp. We believe it's important to give our children the space to build authentic relationships and communication skills with peers—free of all devices.

And because of our willingness to send our kids to the woods without a smartphone, our sons and daughter have plenty of dramatic Kanakuk camp stories. They tell us how they barely survived sailing out in the middle of the lake during a raging storm. Another relives how he and his cabinmate clung for their lives to a tree branch after getting dumped from their canoe into the roaring river. Another tells about the mishaps of overnighting in a cave. Their personal stories go on because we afford our children the opportunity to leave their devices and parents at home and to experience the beauty of living in nature with their peers, tech-free.

STRATEGIES TO CONSIDER

Gathering around the kitchen island, our family laughed our way through the signing of our cell phone contract. Our nearly fourteen-year-old sons and twelve-year-old daughter rolled their eyes before hurriedly initialing every rule for owning the iPhone that their dad and I had agreed to let them buy with their saved money. Our kids figured the sooner they could get that thing signed, the sooner they could get to AT&T to pick out their first phone.

By expressing your family expectations in writing, a cell phone-media contract helps your child balance screen time with real time. We've allowed our children to own smartphones and other technology; therefore, it's our job to teach them how to balance their digital temptations properly. Remember that if you're the one paying for the mortgage, Wi-Fi, and data plans, then you're the one in charge of setting the rules.

Design a Media Contract

Draw up a cell phone contract listing your expectations so that your child can understand that owning a smartphone is a privilege that comes with boundaries. The contract should say something like, "I'm going to let you have a phone, and I will pay for the monthly data IF ...." It's not, "Here is a $400 phone. Go enjoy it!"

Taking the time and making the effort to write out your guidelines shows your child that you are in charge, and that you don't consider technology to be a light matter in your family. Parenting on purpose definitely takes work up front but proactively expressing your expectations will pay off for everyone in the long run.

The positive aspects of designing a media contract for your family include:

- You show your kids that you care about their well-being.

- Your children won't be able to claim that they didn't know or understand that something was a rule or expectation.

- It reminds you, as a parent, about what matters and helps you stick to parenting your values. Likewise, it teaches your kids the importance of matching their online behavior with the values of your family.

- It cuts down on the parental nagging because the expectations and consequences have been clearly stated.

Keep in mind that just because you design a cell phone-media contract and the kids sign it, doesn't mean that it's always going to go smoothly. It won't.

At one point, our daughter was breaking several of our stated family rules. She was draining our family data, downloading apps that we hadn't approved, and regularly taking her phone back to her bedroom, which we've deemed a tech-free zone.

Nagging her and playing the phone confiscation game wasn't working for all involved. So, we pulled out the signed contract and had her highlight the various items that she was not adhering to and asked her to write how she was going to change each behavior before she was allowed her phone back. Having the contract to refer to helped her take ownership of her mistakes and move forward knowing that having an iPhone wasn't free of expectations.

Do she and her brothers still make mistakes and test our family rules? Absolutely.

The goal of a cell phone-media contract is merely to open up a dialogue with kids about our beliefs and values when owning an iDevice. It's not meant to be a harsh, cold, authoritarian document but instead a thoughtful, mindful listing of family expectations and consequences. It is simply a communication tool that is never too late to be introduced to your family, no matter how long your child has already owned a phone.

Check out Appendix C for our family's Cell Phone Contract.

Remain Relevant

Technology can be a positive way to stay in touch and maintain relationships with those we love. Use social media as a way to positively communicate with your child and gain insight into their world.

I am only on Snapchat because my teenagers are. I don't join social platforms to stalk my kids but instead to be relevant to them in a world in which they reside. When I'm traveling, I remain in connection with my kids by sending them quick snaps of my day. It's a way to communicate with one another via the avenue that is authentic to them.

I purposely use my Instagram feed as a way to showcase what I value in my life and what I have going on in my world, so my children can see me for who I am and not just as their mother.

It's important not to use our social media channels as an avenue to highlight our children's lives. Let your child post their achievements and accolades if they want to. Use social media to show your children who you are, not who they already know themselves to be. Remember, your child is watching you, and what you post helps them figure out how they, too, should represent themselves.

GET STARTED TODAY!

It is never too late to pause, pivot, and plan for the changes that you want and need to make as a leader in your family. Reestablish boundaries and communicate with your child today so that they can leave your home better equipped tomorrow.

Pause

What is your present reality?

Do your kids already own devices? Is technology currently a battlefield in your family? Do you have a media contract clarifying your expectations so that your kids understand that owning technology is a privilege?

Pivot

What do you want to keep the same? What do you want to do differently?

Take some time to self-reflect. Do you spend too much time on devices and in front of screens in your family downtime? We must disconnect in order to truly connect with one another; therefore, we must constantly seek out tech-free opportunities for our families. Whether that is a summer camp for the kids or family vacations at campgrounds with poor Wi-Fi, your child never has to know that you planned these screen-free outings on purpose.

Plan

What action can you take to move things in the direction you want to go?

Don't give technology as a gift and then put a set of rules on it. Who wants a gift that comes with boundaries and guidelines? Instead, support your child in purchasing their phone at an appropriate time when they have saved enough money to buy it for themselves.

Remember, there is no need for a child to own a top-of-the-line smartphone, even if they can afford to buy it. Help teach your adolescent that they don't need or deserve the best Apple product on the market. There will be plenty of time as a working adult to purchase the latest and greatest gadgets if that's what they choose to spend their money on later in life.

Want to download my Mindful Media Manifesto or Video Game Expectations? Check out www.AmyCarney.com/Resources and get my list of favorite technology resources as well.

NEXT UP: PARENTS, WE MUST PURPOSELY CREATE RITUALS AND TRADITIONS THAT OUR KIDS WANT TO PUT DOWN THEIR DEVICES FOR.

Chapter 6

Create Meaningful Traditions

I have two glass jars on my kitchen windowsill. They greet me every morning and speak a difficult truth. Nine hundred thirty-six pennies are split unequally between them. What may look like an odd choice of decor above my sink is a purposeful reminder of the fleeting nature of childhood. As I wash the load of dirty dishes each day, I'm visually held accountable for how well I am spending the precious time I've been given with my children. Those penny jars force me to contemplate how well I am investing in my sons' and daughter's childhood.

Lord willing, parents get approximately 936 weeks to raise a child from birth until the age of eighteen. Author Erin Lynum wrote a viral blog post that she expanded into a book on this message of discovering the joys of intentional parenting.[xiii]

The idea is to begin with one glass jar filled with 936 pennies as a tangible reminder of the time we are given to raise our child. Each week, parents purposely remove one penny from the original jar and drop it into the spent one. There is no denying that childhood is short-lived when you have this visual countdown staring you in the face.

With a lump in my throat, I'm forced to accept the reality that very few pennies are left in the original jar. I can now see entirely through the glass which was once blocked by a pile of copper coins. Childhood, in this house, is soon coming to an end. I'm grateful for the painful truth that stares back at me daily, because it reminds me to slow my pace and be intentional with the time I have left with my children under my wing.

Those jars encourage me to continue to honor traditions in our home. I decorate the house each holiday season even though I'm not sure the kids notice anymore. I don't let our crazy schedules distract us from gathering around the table regularly. Each birthday breakfast still begins with the same cinnamon coffee cake, every year. Those jars beg me to make the effort to do what will matter in the end.

How we spend our pennies will write the stories that make up our lives. How we choose to invest our time will determine the details of the childhood we provide for our children.

What is it that you want your child to say when they reflect on growing up in your home? What traditions do you want them to remember and cherish?

WHAT'S THE PROBLEM?

The problem is that, as parents, we are pulled in multiple directions, and our families are busier than ever. We rush around accomplishing, multitasking, and tending to all of the things that our calendar tells us we must do. Yet we must be careful to not be distracted by the urgent disguised as important, or childhood may slip away from us, and we'll find our children walking out the door into adulthood before we ever created the family story we wanted.

Parents, it is our "job" to intentionally take the time and make the effort to cultivate special rituals, also known as traditions, in our home, creating a unique and connective family culture that our kids authentically want to be a part of.

I'm not a big one for working out, but I don't like to miss my Tuesday morning group class at our gym. One day, the regular instructor was out of town, so we had a substitute. Here I was in the same room doing similar poses, but even though the practice was familiar, it felt nothing like our regular class. How could that be?

Our teacher, Shelli, goes above and beyond with the effort she puts into her class. She takes the time to spray various aromatherapy blends throughout our workout. She participates in what she's asking us to do, therefore, becoming one of us. When we lay on our backs in our final resting pose, the lights dim, and battery-operated candles shine around the room. Our nurturing leader then puts a cold, scented towel across each of our closed eyes—a soothing reward for taking care of ourselves for that hour. Shelli's class is always full because she goes beyond the basics of teaching, and her efforts to make the hour matter for her students makes a difference. Her efforts each week make that class somewhere I want to be.

Is growing up in your family an experience that your kids want to be a part of? Is your home somewhere your children want to be?

Childhood will proceed with or without unique rituals, meaningful moments, timeless traditions, or purposeful celebrations. But I guarantee

PARENTS, IT IS OUR "JOB" TO INTENTIONALLY TAKE THE TIME AND MAKE THE EFFORT TO CULTIVATE SPECIAL RITUALS, IN OUR HOME, CREATING A UNIQUE AND CONNECTIVE FAMILY CULTURE THAT OUR KIDS AUTHENTICALLY WANT TO BE A PART OF.

the effort that we put into our family story is what will keep our children showing up in person and staying connected to us when they are no longer living in our home.

Do your efforts make your home a place where your children find connection and comfort away from the stresses of the world? Or are you going through the motions, showing up to lead and love your family like a substitute instructor?

WHAT'S THE SOLUTION?

No matter how hectic life seems to be, we can never get so busy or preoccupied that we forget to take the time to make and continue our unique family rituals and traditions. We must prioritize setting aside sacred time for our family members to gather so that we can celebrate and honor the things that we deem to be most important in life.

Our family story is defined through the daily, weekly, seasonal, and yearly recurring activities that we consciously choose to do with intention and love. Traditions become the anchor of our homes, holding us steady in a complicated world.

"When we start a family tradition that celebrates something we value, a part of us lives on and comes to life every time the family talks about or celebrates that tradition," says Lorle Campos, author of *happyhome*. "It's the simplest and most powerful thing we can do to pass on our cherished values and bring our legacy to life."[xiv]

Traditions are the unique ways we teach values and build family legacies. They are the glue that holds a family together and provides children with comfort because they create predictability in an unpredictable world. *This is us. This is what we do. This is why we do it.*

Create Sacred Spaces

Growing up, I hung out at my best friend Mary's house a lot, and, every once in a while, Mary's mom would send me home because they were about to begin a "family conference"; no outsiders were allowed. As my two feet carried me home, I thought about how their family ritual seemed ludicrous. My parents didn't do this sort of thing in our home, so why in the world would my friend's family need to have meetings when we didn't? As I aged, I began to appreciate the fact that Mary's family set aside sacred time for them and them alone. Did her family value its members more than mine did? Maybe. Maybe not. But they certainly developed an intentional system to connect that my family did not.

In this busy world we live in, how can we be intentional about connecting, face-to-face, with our family members?

Schedule Family Meetings

Holding mindful monthly meetings is a way to slow down and purposefully connect with your family members. These meetings are a relaxed way for everyone to congregate and communicate in person about how things are going within your family unit.

Family meetings are a time to get honest about the strengths and weaknesses of your family and to talk about how well you are living your vision, values, and purpose. Setting aside this sacred time is a way to let your kids know you care about them and the overall health of your entire family.

Family meetings are also a time to coordinate calendars and find out if there are upcoming school projects or supply needs too. We usually enjoy a dessert, and sometimes we even light candles. Make the time fun, relaxed, and productive.

Reframe Family Dinner as Playtime

We've already established how we need more playful moments in our lives, so let's reframe time spent around our family dinner table as a form of healthy play. Research links regular family dinners to better academic performance, higher self-esteem, and a greater sense of resilience as well as lower rates of substance abuse, teen pregnancy, and depression.

"The message for parents couldn't be any clearer. With the recent rise in the number of Americans age 12 and older who are using drugs, it is more important than ever to sit down to dinner and engage your children in conversations about their lives, their friends, school—just talk. Ask questions and really listen to their answers," said Kathleen Ferrigno, CASA's director of marketing who directs the Family Day—A Day to Eat Dinner with Your Children—initiative. "The magic that happens over family dinners isn't the food on the table, but the communication and conversations around it."[xv]

> "THE MAGIC THAT HAPPENS OVER FAMILY DINNERS ISN'T THE FOOD ON THE TABLE, BUT THE COMMUNICATION AND CONVERSATIONS AROUND IT."
> – KATHLEEN FERRIGNO

When our children were young, family dinners were easy. Where else does a seven-year-old have to be on a Tuesday night? That no longer holds true when that same kid grows into a teenager with a driver's license, a job, and a spot on a sports team roster. Seats at the family dinner table can become vacant when you have busy teenagers, so you will most likely have to shift your gathering rituals.

There is nothing so sacred about dinner that other meals can't replace it. To accommodate sports practices and play rehearsals, families may have to eat together at different times, such as breakfast or late-night snacks. Remember, gathering together as often as possible is the goal.

Want to create special dinnertime rituals when your kids are young? Check out Appendix D for ideas!

STRATEGIES TO CONSIDER

Just like my workout instructor purposely turns her class into a unique experience, we too can intentionally create a similar environment for our family by putting the time and effort into developing the loving family culture that we want.

Remember, it's never too late to start creating traditions that correlate with the values that are core to your family. The rituals that you pass down will be a great source of joy and will become the trademark for which your family is known. Here are some ideas to consider:

Establish Annual Traditions

Traditions are a great way to express our creativity and take the time to play together as a family. Year after year, we know what to expect and can anticipate the fun associated with the upcoming holiday or celebration.

It's hanging the same stockings above the fireplace every Christmas season.
It's hiding the same Easter baskets year after year for the children to find.
It's celebrating birthday mornings with the same table decorations.
It's taking the annual first day of school photo in the same spot every year.
It's gathering on the couch and watching your wedding video every anniversary.

Only you know what makes your family unique. Your kids will notice the efforts you make to turn an ordinary childhood into an extraordinary one.

Cultivate Simple Mealtime Rituals

Traditions and rituals don't have to be time consuming or complicated. Cherished and unforgettable moments are possible with the regular practice of showing up to the ordinary. How can we simply make mealtimes more special for our families?

Lawyer, humanitarian, and author Bob Goff and his family have a fun tradition. When they eat dinner on paper plates, a small star is drawn on the bottom of one. It's a big deal to end up with the star plate because the lucky recipient gets to choose the dessert that night. It may be nothing other than a scoop of ice cream or a handful of grapes, but the power comes in the trash talk before discovering who has the winning plate. In the end, everyone wins because they have created a fun, connective ritual in their family.

Lead singers for the band Switchfoot, Jon and Tim Foreman, grew up with their dad making mystery waffles for them on Saturday mornings. Was it going to be Almond Joy, peanut butter, or pineapple and coconut? The winner was the one who could figure out the concoction first. It became a beloved weekend ritual that lasted through junior high.

Professional basketball star Bill Walton used to write John Wooden's motivational quotes on his sons' lunch sacks for school. The four boys and their friends would get a kick out of Dad's efforts.

Connect with Loved Ones

Almost a decade ago, my mom planned an "Asian Day" for our kids complete with handmade decorations, foods, and games. One item she brought to taste test was packaged orange peel, and the consensus was that it was disgusting. I wasn't brave enough to try it, and instead, put my unopened package of the dried Asian delicacy on my mom's pillow to surprise her when she got in bed that night.

The next thing you know, the package of orange peel turned up somewhere when I was least expecting it, and it was game on. In that exchange, our mother-daughter orange peel hiding tradition was born and is still going strong over ten years later. This silly ritual keeps my mom and me connected in our relationship, even though we live across the country from one another. It gives us something to look forward to hiding or finding every time we get together.

Turn Outings into Traditions

Every Father's Day, Dr. Joshua Straub and his dad would attend a Phillies baseball game together, no matter where the team might be playing. The tradition started in 2003 based on the reality that Joshua's dad had congestive heart failure, and they were unsure how much longer he would be around. For thirteen years, father and son were able to keep their tradition alive, until his dad went to heaven. Now Straub honors this Father's Day tradition by taking his son to the games.

Unique practices like these slow us down and remind us who we are as a family. Our rituals celebrate and reinforce the fact that we are loved and that we matter.

Want to make your holiday traditions and family celebrations more meaningful? Go to www.AmyCarney.com/Resources for some simple ideas.

GET STARTED TODAY!

Recommit yourself to cultivating a loving home and connected family. It is never too late to pause, pivot, and plan for the changes that you want and need to make as a leader in your family.

Pause

What is your present reality?

What stands out from your childhood as celebrations or memories of things that you did or experienced in your family growing up? Have you passed any of these traditions down to your kids?

What rituals have you already adopted that you think make your kids feel most connected to your family today?

Pivot

What do you want to keep the same? What do you want to do differently?

Build a large body of traditions to draw from and select those that best fit current needs and realities. What are your daily, weekly, monthly, and seasonal rituals when it comes to holidays? Birthday celebrations? Vacations? Your faith?

Plan

What action can you take to move things in the direction you want to go?

What simple rituals can you create in your home that say to your child that he or she is a unique and essential part of your family? The rituals of your family will change as your children grow. What you did when they were toddlers won't necessarily make sense to do with your teenagers. Shift and create new traditions as your children mature.

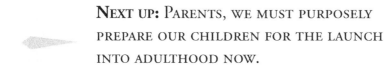

NEXT UP: PARENTS, WE MUST PURPOSELY PREPARE OUR CHILDREN FOR THE LAUNCH INTO ADULTHOOD NOW.

PART 3:

LAUNCH

launch on purpose

 CONTRIBUTE NOT CONSUME
Express Expectations. Create Boundaries.
Embrace Healthy Risks, Failure and Mistakes

RAISE DEVELOP **LIFE SKILLS**
Strong Adults *Coach* instead of coddle

Support instead of *solve* **Redefine**

Teach *Autonomy* **SUCCESS**

Prepare the child for
the path, not the path **Authentically**
FOR THE CHILD serve others

 Make your bed **Develop a good**
Live *with Less* *work ethic*

encourage **Allow**
entrepreneurship *STRUGGLE*

ENGAGE **Build empathy**
in simple service not entitlement

THE WORLD NEEDS CONFIDENT, CAPABLE &
COMPASSIONATE ADULTS - STRIVE TO RAISE THEM

Chapter 7

Develop Life Skills

When I wrote the viral blog post titled "Stop Doing These 8 Things for Your Teen This School Year,"[xvi] I had no idea that writing about instilling life skills in my children would cause so much conversation and controversy. What I thought of as common sense, others deemed to be lazy parenting.

I wrote, "Don't judge me if you happen to see my kids eating packaged Ritz crackers for school lunch. Don't judge me if they're on the sidelines of PE because they forgot their uniform. Don't judge me if they didn't turn in their homework because it's still sitting home on their desk.

What some may view as lack of parenting is what I deem parenting on purpose, working to build necessary life skills in our kids.

How do we raise competent adults if we're always doing everything for our kids? I stopped making daily breakfasts and packing school lunches long ago. I don't feel obligated to deliver forgotten items left behind at home. School projects and homework are not any part of my existence."

One of the 600 comments on that blog post really hit home. The reader posted a reply that said, "Good luck with your tactics working on your adopted son." It made me wonder if having my kids wake up in the morning with an alarm clock, having them wash their own underwear, and having them take charge of their homework were really tactics? I questioned if this reader was right. Would our adopted son, who has some special needs, be unable to learn life skills the way our biological children had?

When our son moved in with us at the age of nine, he wasn't able to handle much responsibility. The group home he had lived in for a couple of years had taught him how to make a perfect bed, but other than that, just tying his shoes or folding the washcloths could bring him to the ground in a puddle of defeat.

Now, less than two years later, he handles his entire morning routine by himself. After school, he does his homework alone and helps with family chores around the house without a problem. As we did with our other children, Keith and I consistently expected him to be a little more capable with each passing day; he slowly developed his everyday skill set without even realizing it. These tasks our son does on his own on a daily basis are not tactics, but they are life skills that actually make him happier and more confident than he's ever been.

Developing life skills is not only good for a child but contributes to the overall health of the family. In an interview I did with Forest Hill Church's Parenting Podcast, I said that we never would have had the emotional space in our family to adopt a child if our four older kids weren't fairly self-sufficient.

I would feel too stressed or too burdened taking care of the children I already had; especially if I was in charge of getting everyone up and out the door every day or having to sit and do homework with them each night, while doing all of the laundry and making all of the meals. When each member of the family takes responsibility for their own lives, it makes our homes run more efficiently, and parenting doesn't become a self-inflicted burden.

Seeking advice for those of us in the season of full-time parenthood, I approached some experts who work alongside young adults every day. I interviewed Arizona college professors, deans, and employers who unanimously stated that the young adults who are making their way onto university campuses and into the work force are, without a doubt, missing crucial life skills. They are missing life skills because we, as parents, are forgetting to teach them.

As parents, it is our "job" to purposely teach our children the life skills today that we want them to leave our home armored with tomorrow.

Phoebe Chalk-Wadsworth has seen a definite shift in her students since she started working at the University of Arizona twenty-seven years ago. Wadsworth is currently the associate athletic director as well as a professor in the sports management undergraduate program. She believes that today's overparenting is hindering her students' abilities to make decisions by themselves. She says,

"Parents are not allowing their children to figure out life on their own."[xvii]

Margaret Nelson, vice dean of Barrett Honors College at Arizona State University, agrees. "The difficulty with working with this generation of kids is that they don't know how to problem-solve. The students, in general, don't come in to solve problems. They want their parents or the dean to do it for them," she said. Nelson adds that she loves it when students come to see her because then she can help them figure out how to solve their issues. "But I can tell that they are disappointed that I'm not just solving it for them," she said. "If students don't learn to problem-solve, it will impede their future."[xviii]

No parent is purposely setting out to impede their child's future, so how is this happening?

> AS PARENTS, IT IS OUR "JOB" TO PURPOSELY TEACH OUR CHILDREN THE LIFE SKILLS TODAY THAT WE WANT THEM TO LEAVE OUR HOME ARMORED WITH TOMORROW.

WHAT'S THE PROBLEM?

"Out of love and desire to protect our children's self-esteem, we have bulldozed every uncomfortable bump and obstacle out of the way, clearing the manicured path we hoped would lead to success and happiness. Unfortunately, in doing so, we have deprived our children of the most important lessons of childhood," said Jessica Lahey, teacher and author of *The Gift of Failure*. "The setbacks, mistakes, miscalculations, and failures we have shoved out of our children's way are the very experiences that teach them how to be resourceful, persistent, innovative, and resilient citizens of this world."[xix]

The problem is we want to raise resourceful, persistent, innovative, and resilient citizens, but we are simply doing too much, thus hindering our child from ever becoming that person. Thanks to modern parenting styles and technology, we are launching kids into adulthood without the proper skills and mindset they need to be successful.

Try to avoid the following parenting styles:

The helicopter parent hovers over their children and swoops in to rescue them at the first sign of trouble. They pay extremely close attention to their child's experiences and problems, particularly at educational institutions. Helicopter parents constantly oversee every aspect of their child's life. Modern technology allows the helicopter parent to hover from great distances. Helicopter parents can give their children directions at any moment, from any location, and can run surveillance on them with various smartphone apps.

The lawnmower parent mows down all of their child's challenges, discomforts, and struggles. They rush ahead to intervene, saving their son or daughter from any potential inconvenience, problem, or discomfort. Lawnmower parents will mow down anyone who might get in the way of their child's perfectly manicured life. These parents constantly communicate with authority figures at school, on the sports field, or in their social circles by emailing their opinions, demands, and advice whenever they feel it necessary.

The concierge parent wants life to run as smoothly as possible, so they remain at their child's beck and call providing all things necessary for a happy life. Like the concierge at a fancy hotel, this parent is happy to cater to their child's every whim, making sure their stay on earth is as perfect as can be. Whatever their child needs, the concierge parent does their best to provide. Modern technology allows the concierge parent to instantly make online purchases for their child as well as provide their son or daughter with apps on their phone to command rides and food delivery services.

Of course, you and I might tend to hover over our children at times. How can we not? Our nature is to nurture, comfort, and caretake. But, the phrase "to nurture" implies growth, so it is vital that we push our children to stand on their own two feet when they are capable of doing so.

All labels aside, the parental behavior we are seeing today can have long-lasting, detrimental effects on a child. If we parent in an overbearing manner, our son or daughter may become ill-equipped to deal with normal life experiences or cope with everyday disappointments. This type of parenting communicates to our child that they aren't capable enough to travel through life alone, and that they cannot be trusted to do things by themselves, which is the farthest thing from the truth.

WHAT'S THE SOLUTION?

We must strive to prepare the child for the path and not the path for the child. "It is not what you do for your children, but what you have taught them to do for themselves, that will make them successful human beings," said Ann Landers.

> "IT IS NOT WHAT YOU DO FOR YOUR CHILDREN, BUT WHAT YOU HAVE TAUGHT THEM TO DO FOR THEMSELVES, THAT WILL MAKE THEM SUCCESSFUL HUMAN BEINGS,"
>
> – ANN LANDERS

Expect Your Child to be Capable

Our goal as a parent is to work ourselves out of a job, which means we must teach our kids what they will need to know before they transition into the real world. We don't want our child to be on a college campus or in the workforce feeling incapable and overwhelmed by everyday responsibilities because we failed to prepare them for real life when they were in our home.

"Everything we want our children to know how to do when they leave our home, they must learn while in our home," said Dr. Deborah Gilboa (Dr. G), parenting and youth development expert and mother of four.[xx]

Do you mistakenly do for your child what they should be doing for themselves because they are busy with their schoolwork and extracurriculars?

Are you too eager to do everything for your children, depriving them of valuable opportunity to learn on their own?

Allow Your Child Space to Struggle

We must help our child build problem-solving and coping skills by allowing them space in their lives to work through everyday complications. Struggle creates strength. Resilience is built from learning and growing from our mistakes, failures, disappointments, and the consequences of our choices.

Let your student feel the discomfort of receiving a low grade when they don't study or forget their homework at home. Conversely, let them experience the pride of a job well done.

Expect your child to stick it out on the team with the "bad" coach or in the class with the "lousy" teacher. Because, unfortunately, the chance of them having a "difficult" roommate or boss one day is highly likely, and we want our son or daughter to be able to handle adversity. Life can be uncomfortable at times and better that our child learns that now rather than later.

Don't fall for the SOS text requests that your children send you throughout the school day. It doesn't mean we love them any less when we say no to bringing them their lunch, PE uniform, or musical instrument. It means we love them enough to know that they need this learning opportunity today more than they need us rescuing them from the uncomfortable moment.

It's time to remove the bubble wrap and let our children experience life's speed bumps as they come their way.

Step Back and Support Not Solve

Like it or not, as our children age, we must allow them to climb into the driver's seat. In the process, we must begin to play a supporting role rather than an active one.

"One of the best things you can do is coach your children to be problem-solvers," said Margaret Nelson of Arizona State University.[xxi]

The problem is that it is sometimes much quicker to just solve the problems that occur for our children because we are smart and efficient people. However, we must purposely slow down and recognize opportunities for our children to solve their own problems that naturally arise throughout adolescence.

Our sixteen-year-old son came home from the mall and announced he had lost his wallet. "What am I supposed to do?" he asked. It is natural for our child's first instinct to be a cry for help: Someone, please fix this problem for me, so I don't have to take the time or worry about how to do it for myself!

Instead of swooping in for the rescue, parents must stop and recognize this as a perfect opportunity to support our child instead of solving the problem for him.

I responded to my son by saying, "I don't know what you should do. What do you think you should do?" Now, of course, I knew what to do, but it's my "job" to help my son learn to problem-solve while he is under my roof. I would not be helping him by giving him the answers.

Instead, I guided him in his thinking by asking a few more questions: What have you done already? What was in your wallet? How are you going to replace those things?

He wasn't sure. So, I gave him space to figure it out—even though it nearly killed my efficient self to watch him problem-solve at a snail's pace. It is not easy to watch our kids struggle through things that we could quickly and easily handle for them.

He made phone calls to the mall security and to the theater to ask if they had found his wallet. No such luck. Then, the following weekend, he asked his dad to drive him to the DMV to replace his license, which he paid for with his own money. Then, he drove to the bank and replaced his debit card and he was back in action.

His mistake = His solution.

It took my son a week to replace everything when I'm pretty sure I could have had the wallet back the same evening that it was lost. But it wasn't my problem to solve; therefore, I had to allow my son the space to come up with his own solution whether I agreed with it or not.

We want our children to know that making mistakes is a fact of life and that they can recover from anything, big or small, that comes their way. Life won't always be perfect, comfortable, and happy, and our children must know and feel that truth.

STRATEGIES TO CONSIDER

Like an academic discipline, life skills need to be taught and practiced. Our kids rely on us to take the time and make the effort to teach them what they are going to need to know when they launch from our homes into adulthood. Teach your child to:

Contribute to the Household

Unfortunately, adult reality includes laundry, making meals, and scrubbing dirty toilets. Better our children grow up learning to accomplish these tasks on a regular basis.

Don't wait until high school to expect your teenager to clean up his room. Begin expecting your toddler to pick up after himself so that this skill naturally develops over time.

Use Their Brain

The other day I was driving my daughter's friend home, and she couldn't tell me where, exactly, she lived. The fourteen-year-old knew her address but couldn't tell me the major cross streets near her house. Her cell phone was dead, and she didn't know her dad's phone number to call him either.

Someone driving our child home shouldn't need Wi-Fi to get them there. Children should memorize their parents' phone numbers and know how to tell an adult where they live without an app. Teens should also know how to navigate the local area without relying on a GPS or smartphone to get around.

Be Responsible for Their Daily Routine

School-age children should be able to use an old-school alarm clock to wake them up in the morning. While we will prepare our children's meals on most days, there is no reason why they can't learn to pack their own snacks and school lunches as they get older.

Our kids should also learn to pack what they need in their own backpacks for school and in their bags for sports, camp, or vacation. The more you hold your child responsible for their own tasks, the more responsible they will become—on most days.

Self-Advocate

We aren't helping our son or daughter when we email, call, and text teachers, coaches, and other adults in authority on our child's behalf. When our child says their teacher has done them wrong, we must listen to them and have empathy.

But we must not jump in, undermine the adult in charge, and solve our child's issue for them. Instead, we must coach our child by teaching them how to speak up for themselves and communicate with adults in a positive way through appropriate channels.

GET STARTED TODAY!

Recommit yourself to focusing your parental efforts on raising an adult. It is never too late to pause, pivot and plan for change. Reestablish boundaries and communicate with your child to help them become the strong adult the world needs.

Pause

What is your present reality?

Get honest with yourself and your parental leadership. Have you been striving to prepare your child for the path or the path for your child?

Pivot

What do you want to keep the same? What do you want to do differently?

What can you teach your child today that will help them become the adult you want to launch tomorrow? Write a list of responsibilities you would like to hand over to your child and then schedule a family meeting to discuss this shift.

Plan

What action can you take to move things in the direction you want to go?

Start simple by teaching your child how to do everyday tasks around your home.

"Start each day by making your bed," said Naval Admiral William H. McRaven. "Making your bed will reinforce the fact that the little things matter. If you can't do the little things right, you will never be able to do the big things right. If you want to change the world, start off by making your bed." It doesn't get any simpler than that.[xxii]

Check out Appendix E for an age-appropriate list of chores and life skills!

NEXT UP: PARENTS, WE MUST PURPOSELY STRENGTHEN OUR CHILD'S WORK ETHIC AND FINANCIAL SKILLS.

Chapter 8

Raise Grounded Kids

Our family was at a surprise, sweet sixteen party awaiting the birthday girl's arrival when the friend next to me pointed to the decorated SUV in front of us and said, "Can you believe that you are going to have to buy three of those soon?"

Three cars? She couldn't be serious. Was this friend implying that we were supposed to buy our triplet sons cars for their sixteenth birthday?

Although we were several years away from this milestone, I knew that purchasing vehicles as gifts for our children wasn't going to happen. We say no, not because we can or can't afford it, but because we know that saying no is what's best for our child in the long run.

Back in high school, I couldn't talk my working parents into buying the pair of Gloria Vanderbilt jeans that I wanted. Growing up, my mom and dad provided for me, but they didn't indulge me. Therefore, I had to find a way to indulge myself, which meant going to work at Burger King at the age of fifteen. I was finally able to get my jeans and felt proud that I was able to buy them with my own money. Not only could I begin to purchase and do things that I wanted, I also began, more importantly, to develop a strong work ethic that continues today.

What if my parents had bought me the jeans?

They would have saved me the embarrassment of wearing those navy polyester pants and maroon polo shirt with the coordinating visor and spending my Friday nights in that fast food restaurant—instead of at the high school football games where I would have liked to have been. My mom and dad would have "saved me" from learning that buying designer jeans takes hard work and sacrifice.

Fast forward to today. My husband and I are raising our children in a privileged community, unlike those in which either of us was raised. How could Keith and I teach our children the lifelong lessons and timeless values surrounding money and hard work that we wanted them to have amidst the culture of affluence in which we live? Easily—by purposely saying no to buying the things that our kids want but can't afford themselves, by expecting our children to work to earn their own money, and by expecting them to be contributors in our household and in the world.

Each generation of adults enjoys telling stories about how hard they had it growing up compared to how good their children have it now. We talk about how we had to go to work at a young age and ride our bike miles across town to get where we wanted to go. Our parents didn't regularly buy us things or take us places.

We tell stories from our latchkey kid days and talk about the times we had to walk to school in the pouring rain or freezing snow. Our parents weren't always there to make sure we were happy and comfortable.

Yet, you and I know the trials and tribulations we experienced in childhood are the very things that developed us into the strong, resilient, hardworking adults we are today. I'm afraid that the privileged children we're raising in this generation won't have any woeful childhood tales to tell their kids.

I often hear parents complain about how their teenager doesn't have the same motivation, drive, or work ethic that they, themselves, had as an adolescent.

One evening, I was sitting on the YMCA bleachers watching my sons' basketball game, when the mom next to me talked of her frustrations with her son not wanting to get his driver's license or a job. "He's just not interested. I don't know why. All he wants to do is play video games," she said.

I encouraged her to push her son to do what she knew would be good for him regardless of whether he felt like he wanted to do those things or not.

Isn't this what we nice and loving parents do today? We say, "Well, if little Johnny doesn't feel like doing it, I guess he doesn't have to," and then later we question why in the world Johnny doesn't have the strong work ethic or motivation that we had at that same age. Go figure.

When our kids turned sixteen, Keith and I didn't care if they felt like driving or not. Getting a driver's license at that age was the expectation in our family. We weren't interested in how our teens felt about getting a part-time job and paying for their own gas or cell phone bill either.

We, as parents, must be willing to push our children to do the things that will help them grow into the capable and confident adults we want them to be. Allowing them to sit home and play video games, instead of going to work, isn't going to create the same outcome.

A few weeks after that conversation in the bleachers, my son came home and told me his friend said that I had "ruined his life." He was now in driver's education classes, had a job bagging groceries at the local grocery store, and had limited access to the video game system. I was so happy that his mom was courageous enough to act on the things she had wanted for her son because he will be better off in the long run because of her guidance.

If we want to launch hardworking adults, we must create opportunities for our kids to work hard during their childhood.

If we want to raise resilient adults, we must let our sons and daughters struggle to do things they don't necessarily want to do or that might prove difficult for them in the moment.

If we want to launch responsible adults, we must give our children responsibilities.

We must remember the end goal for our sons and daughters and then not be afraid to help them get there.

WHAT'S THE PROBLEM?

The problem lies in our quest to create a beautiful and happy childhood. As parents, we mistakenly buy, do, and give too much while expecting very little of our children in return.

We see twelve-year-olds walking around with smartphones with data plans purchased by their parents. Teenage girls without jobs are on regular beauty regimes getting waxed, highlights in their hair, or their nails done—all on their parents' dime. Teenagers and young adults (where we live) regularly command rides and order food from apps attached to their parents' credit cards.

Why are we allowing our children to enjoy adult privileges without working to pay for them?

Why Teens Aren't Working Today

Alex Apodaca and his team own over sixty Dunkin Donuts franchises in four different states, and he says that his two locations in north Scottsdale, Arizona, are the hardest to staff because of the area's affluence.[xxiii]

Teenagers from privileged homes don't have to work, so they aren't choosing to, and parents aren't encouraging or expecting them to work either.

The presence of teenagers in the summer workforce in July 1978 was at 72 percent. A recent report by the Pew Research Center analyzed the average summer employment rate for 16- to 19-year-olds in June, July, and August 2017, and found that only 35 percent of teens worked a summer job.[xxiv]

Many teenagers are not choosing to get jobs because they want to focus on other activities that they think might better impress college admissions officers, such as sports, music, student council, and volunteering.

Our kids are overscheduled and under so much pressure to achieve that they don't have time to babysit on the weekend or hold a part-time job that can teach them more about life than any class or organized activity ever will.

The pressure to get into a top university keeps our kids focused on personal performance in the classroom and in extracurricular activities. Parents feel sorry for their busy child because there is so much on their plate, so they do not ask them to help around the home or to contribute financially to any of their personal needs or desires. This is where, as parents, we are going wrong—if our child is too busy to contribute, then they should be too busy to consume.

So, what do you do if it seems like everyone around you is purchasing new cars and expensive gadgets for their children? Though it won't be easy, be courageous enough to purposely deprive your child of things that don't align with your values, even when your entire community seems to endorse it. Parenting on purpose can and will, sometimes, be difficult.

We do not deny our child to be mean; we deny them to teach life skills, lessons, and values that will serve them well in adulthood. Our "job" as a parent is not to indulge, entitle, entertain, and make our child happy. As parents, our "job" is to purposely raise our child to be a strong adult that can confidently go out into the world with the ability to work hard for what they want.

When parents buy their teens a car and pay for the expenses that go along with the privilege of driving, they teach their children that all they have to do is show up and receive. When we allow our teenager to drive our family car and expect them to pay for some of the costs—insurance, oil changes, and gas—we teach our child that privileges come with responsibility.

> **AS PARENTS, OUR "JOB" IS TO PURPOSELY RAISE OUR CHILD TO BE A STRONG ADULT THAT CAN CONFIDENTLY GO OUT INTO THE WORLD WITH THE ABILITY TO WORK HARD FOR WHAT THEY WANT.**

Just because you work hard and can afford a comfortable lifestyle as an adult, doesn't mean you should hinder your child from learning the same values and work ethic that enabled you to earn the standard of living that you now enjoy.

How can we better raise hardworking and grounded kids in our culture of excess?

WHAT'S THE SOLUTION?

Expect Your Child to Work

We expected our sons to pay for their own gas while driving our family car. This meant they needed to find part-time work on the weekends, so they got jobs in a local breakfast restaurant hosting and bussing tables. We are fortunate that the manager is accommodating about working around their busy schedules.

Not only are our kids earning money, they are also learning interpersonal, communication, and problem-solving skills. Dealing with a boss teaches them the ability to accept and learn from criticism. Being responsible, meeting challenges, and demonstrating good work habits builds self-confidence as well.

Live with Less

If we don't want to raise materialistic adults, we must diminish the power of materialism in our homes. Show your child that you don't need to own the latest device or drive a luxury car. Our spending habits are a direct correlation of what we value in life, and your children see how you choose to spend your money.

Where do your children see you purposely save money? Especially in an unpredictable economy, it's important that we model what it looks like to be able to afford things yet choose not to buy them.

Teach Your Child to Manage Their Money

Help your child open a bank account when they are young and then, eventually, attach it to their own checkbook or debit card. Besides helping them manage their account online, teach your child how to go into a bank branch and talk to the teller. If our children are going to make money, then they need to learn to manage it as well.

Another opportunity to learn about budgeting might be to have a high schooler pay the family bills and balance the checkbook for a few months. The teen will be paying bills and balancing checkbooks for the rest of his or her life so better they learn how to do it now.

STRATEGIES TO CONSIDER

Give a Consistent Allowance

Consider giving your child a monthly allowance as a way to learn how to manage money instead of paying them for their performance or chores. Make sure the allotted allowance you provide also comes with a list of items that you will no longer pay for—such as meals out with friends, birthday gifts, haircuts, cell phone data, or food for their pet hamster.

Giving a child an allowance isn't about handing them free money, it's about letting our sons or daughters learn how to navigate their saving and spending habits while they are in our home.

One day, our daughter went to the water park with her friends. When she came home, she said she couldn't believe how expensive it was. We want our child to have the opportunity to feel the pain of spending their own money on experiences or material items they want. She would never have known that the water park ticket was expensive if we had continued to pay for it.

Encourage Entrepreneurship Early

Instill a strong work ethic and an entrepreneurial mindset in your children at a young age. Brainstorm ideas with your son or daughter on how they can earn money. Years ago, my husband and sons created an eBay business reselling name brand athletic shoes they had purchased from Nordstrom's Last Chance Clearance Store. With their dad's help, an online store was something they were able to create before they were of legal working age. As busy teenagers, they are still able to do this during the school year when they don't have the availability to work their regular job.

When fidget spinners were the craze, our boys bought a hundred of them from a wholesaler in China and sold them in a week. Another son scoured thrift shops and book resellers for high school summer reading books and sold them for a profit. Our daughter likes to clean, organize, and babysit for people to earn her money.

What passion or skill does your child have that they can profit from?

Create Mindful Spending Habits

Raise your child with a frugal mindset, regardless of your financial status. Teach your child that they don't always need the best, even if they can afford it.

Check the local used bookstore or the library for that book they need for English class before ordering it from Amazon. Not only do you teach your child delayed gratification and to save money by going to a secondhand shop, you also model the importance of supporting local businesses.

Help your child recycle bottles and cans or sell their used books or outgrown clothes to consignment shops for extra cash. Raise your son or daughter with an understanding that helping our environment also helps our bank accounts.

GET STARTED TODAY!

Recommit yourself to your vision, values, and purpose. Reestablish boundaries and communicate with your child. It is never too late to pause, pivot, and plan for the changes that you want and need to make as a leader in your family.

Pause

What is your present reality?

Is there entitlement in your home? What expectations do you have for your child when it comes to making and managing money? What items do you purposely say no to that you could afford but aren't willing to buy for your child?

Pivot

What do you want to keep the same? What do you want to do differently?

Do you currently give an allowance as a way for your child to begin to learn how to manage money? Do you expect your child to get a job to help pay for the privileges that he or she has in their life or are you mistakenly indulging them with too much?

What can your child begin to pay for with their own money?

Plan

What action can you take to move things in the direction you want to go?

Be willing to help your child start a business of their own. What can they sell at a local farmers market, on eBay, or on social media with your help? Who do you know that may be willing to hire your teen for their first job?

NEXT UP: PARENTS, WE MUST PURPOSELY PROVIDE OPPORTUNITIES FOR OUR CHILD TO AUTHENTICALLY SERVE OTHERS.

Chapter 9

Redefine Success

As I walked alone around the impoverished Yucatan village, I began to question my purpose for being there. Our family was on another medical mission trip with our dentist, and while everyone else seemed to have an important role to play, I was left wondering why I hadn't gone to medical school, so I could be of better use here.

I wandered through the dusty square taking water to my family members. Keith labored alongside a group of men constructing a new playground in the center of the village. Our daughter was in her element at the vacation bible school doing crafts and playing with all of the local children. Two of our sons stood outside the public restrooms, in the scorching summer sun, testing urine samples for diabetic patients.

As I made my way through our team's makeshift clinic, I came across my rough and tough, hockey-playing teenage son kneeling on the dirty tile, washing the feet of an elderly woman waiting her turn to see the doctors. It became clear to me that I didn't need to go to medical school to be of use. I only needed to be a mom willing to replace our family's entertaining summer vacation with an uncomfortable service trip to Valladolid, Mexico. I realized that it was my "job" to lead my children to this place, affording them the opportunity to humbly serve others in a way that our daily life doesn't allow.

Parents, it is "our job" to provide our children with the experiences that will help them develop into the caring and compassionate people they are meant to become. They need our willingness to prioritize spending our precious resources on serving others rather than continually serving ourselves. We can't force our children to care about others, but we can certainly put prompts and possibilities before them that will increase their odds of caring. It is up to us to engage our kids in a story bigger than themselves.

As parents, our "job" is to provide our children with the experiences that will help them develop into the caring and compassionate people they are meant to become.

Going on those family mission trips to Valladolid, Mexico, instead of Disneyland, writes the scenes of the story that Keith and I want our lives and legacy to tell. We want to be people who serve God and others before serving ourselves. Therefore, we have to carve out space in our lives to do this authentically.

Back home, on a day-to-day basis, I strive to make sure my children know that even though their effort to achieve good grades and improve their sports game is important, what matters, even more, is how they choose to help the people around them to the best of their ability every day of their lives. I want to raise my sons into adults who will stop and help a motorist who has broken down on the side of the road or simply offer to help a traveler stow a heavy suitcase into the overhead bin on the airplane.

I want my children to see the needs of the world and strive to fill them without someone telling them they should do so. I hope my sons and daughter see hurt, pain, and suffering, whether next door or overseas, and do their part to relieve it.

When Keith and I claimed our values and composed our parenting purpose statement, we said that we wanted to raise kind, compassionate, loving, and empathetic people. We wanted to raise our children in an outward focused home that served people on a regular basis. We wanted a family that would impact the lives and the world around us. We wanted to be a family where serving others is who we are, not what we do. But, how could we prioritize these desires when our daily reality was consumed with opportunities to serve ourselves?

We accomplished this by redefining the meaning of success for our family.

The Merriam-Webster dictionary defines success as achieving wealth, power, or fame.[xxv] We see this definition playing out in popular culture around us all of the time.

When Keith and I stop and define success for our children and our family, it doesn't look anything like social status or the acquisition of expensive material items. Success is walking through that makeshift diabetes clinic in the impoverished Yucatan village and witnessing our teenage son on his knees washing the feet of strangers. Seeing our children humbly serve the Lord = Success to us.

Success is watching our biological kids wrestle, tickle, laugh, and love on their younger adopted brother. Loving sibling bonds = Success to us.

Success is seeing our children, even as teenagers, laugh and enjoy spending time with their grandparents, aunts, and uncles. Strong family relationships = Success to us.

How do you define success in your family?

WHAT'S THE PROBLEM?

The problem is performance-driven parenting. In popular culture today, many moms and dads devote their time, energy, and money to helping their child succeed. Parents today want their children in the best schools, with the best teachers, in the best classes, and getting the best grades. Mom and Dad want their child on the best teams and in the best clubs, and the race is on to get their child into the best college that they can.

Compounding this issue is that we rarely stop to define what our "best" looks like. We take popular culture's definition of success and run with it whether it works for our own family or not.

Another problem lies with the mandatory service requirements that some schools and organizations now require of their students. What began as a great idea to get adolescents involved with the community has turned into one more item, we now add to the list of things we have to do. Parents have been told that volunteering looks good on the college application, so they begin to seek out service opportunities for their child to meet the requirements. Serving becomes another "thing" we strive to accomplish.

When our sons were in eighth grade, they struggled to meet the service hours required for National Junior Honor Society because we were focused on fostering a little boy whom we planned to adopt. I wasn't able to schedule or drive my kids to community service opportunities outside of our home during that time.

At the end of the school year, our kids were embarrassed and upset with me when they didn't have enough hours documented on their NJHS log. I wrote an email to the teachers heading up the organization to explain why our kids had fallen short—because we were busy caring for a foster child in our home.

I never heard anything back from those adults in charge, so I'm not sure if they were okay with the truth or if our children were removed from the society. Though it was an uncomfortable life lesson for the kids, we explained to them that we were prioritizing what was important for our family, not an organization. Meeting the needs of this child living in our home was more important than aimlessly serving somewhere in the community to fulfill necessary hours. It is important that we teach our children the difference between mandated volunteering and authentic service.

Sincerity Matters

I read about a student who listed his impressive local volunteer work and his out-of-the-country service trips on his college application, but when admissions asked him if he helped make meals at home or did his laundry, the answer was no. Did he support a neighbor or regularly take care of a younger sibling? The answer again was no. He was not accepted because the university felt he wasn't sincere in his service.

One of the required essay questions on MIT's undergraduate application reflects its commitment to student contributions to the public good. The app now asks students to describe one way in which they have contributed to their community—whether in the family, the classroom, the neighborhood, etc.

Maybe we should start with that simple college essay prompt. How easy would it be for your child to sit down and authentically write that essay from their heart and experience?

Are you leading your son or daughter to serve others authentically or merely to check something off their to-do list?

It's easy to get caught up in culture's definition of success and forget to allow space in your lives for the significant things that will genuinely build the character and loving heart you want your kids to have. We must be intentional about creating opportunities for our children so that they can become the type of people that will bring value to the world around them.

How do we make community service an authentic part of our busy lives, instead of squeezing in our volunteer time because we think it will look good on a college application or resume?

WHAT'S THE SOLUTION?

We must take the time to redefine success for our families and then make space in our week to authentically serve others. "Service is the rent we pay for being. It is the very purpose of life and not something you do in your spare time," according to Marian Wright Edelman, founder and president of The Children's Defense Fund.[xxvi]

> "SERVICE IS THE RENT WE PAY FOR BEING. IT IS THE VERY PURPOSE OF LIFE AND NOT SOMETHING YOU DO IN YOUR SPARE TIME."
>
> – MARIAN WRIGHT EDELMAN

Build Empathy Instead of Entitlement

Children are born with the capacity for empathy, but it needs to be nurtured throughout their lives. Learning empathy is like learning a language or a sport; it requires practice and guidance.

Empathy is, at its simplest, an awareness of the feelings and emotions of other people. It is a crucial element of emotional intelligence, or the link between self and others. Empathy is more than just understanding what others are experiencing; it's almost as if we are feeling the experience ourselves.

If we want to raise empathetic kids, we must be willing to take the time and make the effort to create space in their lives for opportunities that will build empathy rather than an impressive resume.

Value People Over Possessions

We set the standards for our children, so they must first see their mother or father willing to live a life of sacrificial service to others. Figure out what you are passionate about and allow your kids to participate. If your passion is your children, then it won't be such a stretch to expand that passion to other children who don't have the advantages that yours do.

The Lord has immensely blessed our family; therefore, we wanted to share our blessings with other children by doing foster care, which eventually led to mentoring and adoption.

"Your children will never move toward honoring others until they genuinely believe that you value people over things," said Dave Stone in his book, *How to Raise Selfless Kids in a Self-Centered World.*[xxvii]

What do your kids see you value? Where do they see you spend your money and time?

In the Bible, Matthew 6:21 says "for where your treasure is, there your heart will be also." Therefore, I don't want my children to see me value material possessions or worldly success. I want them to see me bravely loving and helping people on a consistent basis. Hopefully, my heart for serving others will transfer to my children.

STRATEGIES TO CONSIDER

Engage in Simple Daily Acts of Service

Learning to serve begins at home. How consistently do you help one another in your house? Do the kids contribute to the household duties, or do they get to live as guests in your home? Once a child helps out at home, he or she can evolve into helping out in the community. It doesn't mean much if your son or daughter is out serving in the community but struggles to help in your family and home.

Include your children in the experience of serving others daily. Teach children to push shopping carts left in the parking lot back up to the store on your way in and to hold doors open for other people in public. Help a neighbor by bringing their newspaper up to the front door.

Always model how you can help make someone's life easier. When eating out in restaurants, teach your children to clean up the table, lessening the work for the server. Practice hospitality by inviting people into your home as a way to show your children how to care for other people.

Simply strive to make life easier for someone else regularly.

Create a Family Giving Plan

Too many times, as parents, we do all the giving without involving our kids in a discussion about how much we give, who we give to, and why we do it. Kids often don't have the opportunity to learn about what social causes are important to them because it's not brought to their attention. Get the kids involved in the process and discuss where your family can give of your time, treasures, and talents.

Here are a few questions to get you started:

What cause(s) are you are interested in serving, and how can you go about filling the needs of that community?

Who are you drawn to serving? Is it the poor and hungry? The homeless and those living on the streets? Is it those with special needs, or pets and animals living in shelters? Is it our wounded military veterans or finding a cure for a disease that has touched your family?

Develop an Authentic Service Journey

Figure out who you are drawn to serving and then help that group of people with purpose and passion. Let your service authentically evolve over the years.

Are you currently reacting to the open slot on your calendar and filling it with whatever service opportunity happens to be available? To transform and impact lives, figure out what cause or group of people pull at your heartstrings and then serve them. Sacrifice for them. Get uncomfortable so they can become comfortable.

I've chosen a journey of advocating for children in foster care. As someone who grew up in a safe home with a family who loved me, I can't fathom that there are thousands of abused and neglected children living in our country without loving adults to take care of them.

My passion and desire to help these kids has led our family to do foster care, respite care, and adoption. Also, I have mentored foster teens and currently speak and write about our foster care journey to adoption to bring awareness to the needs of these vulnerable children.

When our kids were young, Keith and I said that we wanted an outward-focused family who would make a difference in the world. If that's what we want, then that's what we have to act on. We can't allow our excuses to stop us from doing hard, but significant things.

GET STARTED TODAY!

Recommit yourself to your vision, values, and purpose. It is never too late to make a change. Give your children something better to aim toward than where they might be headed today.

Pause

What is your present reality?

Do you log the hours your child volunteers as a requirement for school or another organization? If so, would you continue to serve in the community without this requirement?

Do your children see you sacrifice your time, treasures, and talents for the good of others?

Pivot

What do you want to keep the same? What do you want to do differently?

Make serving others a priority in your home.

Make a purposeful plan to distribute your time, funds, and tangible treasures between organizations and authentic causes you want to support in your local community, nationally, and globally. Get the kids involved in deciding where you will donate your time, money, and unwanted goods.

Plan

What action can you take to move things in the direction you want to go?

As a family, perhaps you could save money for a less fortunate child to go on a special outing that they couldn't otherwise afford. For example, summer camp is a blessing we give to our children, so we want to give a similar experience to a child who may not be able to attend without our help; therefore, Keith and I have chosen to sponsor kids to attend weeklong, sleepaway summer camps through Kids Across America because this is an authentic fit for our family.

NEXT UP: PARENTS, WE MUST LIVE OUT THE LEGACY TODAY THAT WE WANT TO LEAVE BEHIND TOMORROW.

Conclusion

Live Out Your Legacy

One ordinary afternoon, as my aunt and I were leisurely shopping at a Phoenix strip mall, I received a call on my cell phone from an unknown number. Since I was in a good mood, I went ahead and answered it, oblivious to the life-changing truth I was about to hear. It wasn't the random sales call I thought it would be; instead, it was the nurse from my gynecologist's office letting me know that the results of my recent appointment were not good. The tests had detected cervical cancer, and it was at a stage that would require an immediate hysterectomy. When could I come in?

One minute, I was leisurely searching for healthy snacks for my kids' school lunches, and the next minute I was preparing for surgery. How could this be possible?

Because this is life, and anything is possible.

Those next few minutes, weeks, and months were a blur.

Me? Cancer? I had always been a healthy person overall, so being told in 2011 that I had cancer came as quite a shock. During this unsettling period, I asked myself if I would have regrets if I were to die from this disease. Was I living and loving people in my life the way I wanted to? Had I prepared the keepsakes and mementos that I wanted to leave behind for my children if it were, in fact, my time?

I will never forget the peace that came over me knowing that, whether I would live or die, I was going to do it with little regret. The Lord, thankfully, spared me from that disease, but He also made me more alive to the preciousness of life.

Our lives can and might change in an instant.

After my cancer diagnosis, I knew that I did not want to get to the end of full-time parenthood, or my overall life, and wish that I had put in more effort or had lived life more courageously. That was when I recommitted to live my life and parent my children *on purpose*, because I would only get one chance at both.

I will end this book with the same truth as it began—we must parent and live our lives from the end. Not only must we look toward our child's high school graduation and parent toward that vision, but even more importantly, we must visualize our deathbed and make choices about today with the end in mind.

What regrets would you have if you were to die next week, month, or year? Would this insight change anything about how you live today?

Our calendars don't lie, and neither will our obituary, funeral, or celebration of life. How we spend our precious time in this one life we've been given matters. How we choose to parent our child in this one season of childhood matters. How we purposely decide to lead, love, and launch our child matters.

We falsely believe that we can make the scrapbooks and take the vacations and get to all of the things we want to do—later. I hope that the Lord will provide us with later, but tomorrow is not a guarantee.

When we die, no one will care what type of house we lived in, what car we drove, or what Pinterest-worthy parties we threw or attended. No one will talk about our beautiful clothes or the fine wine we drank or served either. Our lives and our legacy will be measured by what we gave to others, not what we received or owned.

"Legacy is organizing the way you live your life so that you will be a blessing to other people for generations to come," according to Phil Munsey, author of *Legacy Now*. "It's nothing more than taking the responsibility to ensure that your relationships and resources will outlive and outlast your time here on earth."[xxviii]

Our legacies are slowly built, one decision at a time. Knowing this, Keith and I were able to say yes to taking our RV family sabbatical around the USA. It's why we said yes to foster care and adoption. It's why we say yes to taking regular mission trips to the Yucatan to serve as a family. It's why we continue to make courageous choices to create the life we want to live today, and the legacy we want to leave behind tomorrow.

A couple of years ago, my friend Jacqui and I stood on the high school bleachers chatting as our sons warmed up before their basketball game. Jacqui told me she was upset that her family had to cancel their cruise vacation because the team had scheduled a tournament over the holiday break.

Not knowing that cancer was raging through her body at the time, I looked her in the eye and asked, "If you knew you were going to die soon, would you go on that cruise?" And she said, "Yes," but then added, "At least we will save money if we decide not to go." I told her that, yes, she would save money, but that she wouldn't be able to take that with her when she dies either. She still canceled the family vacation.

And guess what? Jacqui died less than a year and a half after we had that conversation. I still can't believe that the Lord put it on my heart to speak that truth to her about taking that family vacation when neither of us had any idea she would soon suffer from a rare form of liver cancer that would end up taking her life. (You can read more about this in a blog post I wrote shortly after our original talk, "You are Dying. Live Like It.")[xxix]

As Jacqui weakened through her cancer treatments, she didn't have the energy to begin making the keepsakes that she had wanted to make for her three school-aged sons. She had wanted to do more. She had meant to do more. She just ran out of time.

Don't run out of time, my friend. Create the memorable moments, the lasting memories, and the meaningful keepsakes now. Print the pictures. Write the stories. Be proactive and draw up the important legal paperwork that needs to be prepared. Take the time to do the tangible things you need and want to leave behind.

Life is a journey, not a destination.

Parenthood is a marathon, not a sprint.

Slow down, enjoy your race, and keep in mind that the finish line is somewhere ahead.

Are you living the life you want today and creating the legacy you wish to leave behind tomorrow?

Take the time and make the effort to live and parent on purpose today.

Our Parenting Purpose Statement

#parentinggoals

Here's how Keith and I answered the questions in chapter three, to determine our parenting purpose.

- **We don't want a family who** aimlessly lives life with no direction. Is disconnected. Constantly argues. Is stagnant and boring.

- **We will not raise children who** are privileged and entitled amidst this affluent world we are raising them in. We will not raise children who are self-serving and consumed by materialism and worldly success.

- **We will not launch adults who** are victims to circumstances or other people. Are dependent on us. Aren't confident enough to make their own decisions. Wander aimlessly through life. Are irresponsible and entitled.

- **We don't want a home where** people can't be themselves. Yelling, fighting, and sarcasm are normal. It's stuffy and serious.

OUR PARENTING PURPOSE

First and foremost, we will not lose ourselves to our roles of mother and father but will instead prioritize our roles as children of God and as husband and wife. We will strive to lead our children to be the best version of themselves while modeling our convictions in our own lives.

- **We want a family who** is made up of unique and interesting individuals who are in an interdependent relationship with one another. We depend on one another, yet we aren't dependent on each other.

- **We want to raise children who** are loyal and loving siblings who forgive and laugh with one another on a regular basis. We want to raise kids who love life and others. We want our sons and daughter to know the value of authentic relationships, strong community, and meaningful experiences.

- **We want to launch adults who** are faith-filled as well as fun loving, adventurous, confident, courageous, independent, responsible, kind, compassionate, respectful, intelligent, humble, and hard working.

- **We want a home where** laughter and love abound and where people feel secure and supported in being themselves. We want a comfortable home where reminders of who we are surround us through what hangs on our walls and graces our shelves.

APPENDIX B
List of 92 Values and Virtues

Adventurous	Disciplined	Healthy
Appreciative	Energetic	Helpful
Assertive	Engaging	Honest
Authenticity	Enthusiastic	Honor
Brave	Entrepreneurial	Humble
Caring	Excellence	Imagination
Charitable	Fair	Independent
Compassionate	Faith	Individualistic
Committed	Flexible	Innovative
Community	Forgiving	Integrity
Confident	Friendly	Intentional
Considerate	Fun	Joyful
Cooperative	Generous	Justice
Courageous	Gentle	Kind
Courteous	Grit	Leadership
Creative	Growth	Limitless
Curious	Happy	Love
Determined	Hard Work	Loyalty

Meaningful	Playful	Service
Mindful	Polite	Significant
Moderation	Positive	Spiritual
Modest	Present	Steadfast
Moral	Proactive	Stewardship
Obedient	Productive	Supportive
Optimistic	Protective	Thankful
Orderly	Purposeful	Thrifty
Passionate	Reliable	Tolerance
Patient	Respect	Trustworthy
Peaceful	Responsible	Truthful
Persistent	Reverent	Unique
Perseverance	Self-disciplined	

APPENDIX C

Our Family Cell Phone Contract

Mom and Dad trust you or we would not let you have a phone, therefore we will not make a daily habit of checking it. Your phone is your personal business and we trust that you will be making good choices and decisions with your conversations and communications.
That being said, we do have the following expectations for owning your phone…

We must know your password at all times and we have the right to check your phone any time we feel it is necessary.

I will continue to do my best in all aspects of my life– school, sports, activities, etc.
If your phone distracts you from doing your schoolwork or meeting other obligations, you will hand it over so that you are better able to concentrate on what's important.

My phone will be taken away if any character issues arise.
If we hear of any inappropriate texts, calls, pictures, etc. we will have to take your phone until we can sit down and talk it through.

I will not lie about what I'm doing on my phone.
Dishonesty breaks down trust and we won't be able to let you continue to carry around a device that is causing you to deceive people. This includes deleting text strings.

I will be respectful of the family data plan that we are all sharing.
If you go over your allotted amount of time, your data will be shut off until the billing cycle starts over.

I will always communicate with members of the opposite sex with respect.
Do not text, email or say anything through this device that you wouldn't say in person. Remember that most likely their parents will be reading what you are saying and looking at your photos. Conduct yourself appropriately.

If I receive something uncomfortable or dangerous from a friend, I am expected to bring it to my parents attention.
It is not okay to ignore someone's cry for help.

I will follow the rules that my school has in place for cell phones at all times.

{2}

_____ **Be present. Be in the now.**
Be able to put your phone away and enjoy real time conversations with your family and friends. You are not a rude person, so don't let this piece of technology change you.

_____ **My phone must be placed in the agreed upon area each evening at bedtime.**
Respect other families by not texting or calling well before this time!

_____ **Be a good friend and always remember to individualize your friendships.**
Do not assume that a friend feels value in what you may say in a group text. Be sure to have separate interactions as well. Don't ever involve yourself in conversations that are hurtful to others.

_____ **I will not respond to or reply to any communication from unknown contacts.**

_____ **My parents have the right to monitor all apps and have me delete any that they deem inappropriate.**
Just because your friends are using something, doesn't mean that it's okay for our family. You will need to respect our decisions as we will have done our research.

_____ **Everything I do and say online is subject to judgement and makes up my reputation.**
Do not use this technology to lie or deceive another person. Your reputation is a piece of our family reputation. Always be your best self.

_____ **Purposely leave your phone at home sometimes.**
Learn to live without your device, as it's not an extension of you.

_____   _____
Child Signature/Date   Parent Signature/Date

This is an exciting time and we are so proud of you for waiting patiently until Mom and Dad felt it was the right time for you to own your first cell phone!

May your relationships with your friends and family strengthen through the ability to text and reach out to one another on this device!

We love you dearly!
• • • • • • • • • • • • • • • • •
- www.parentonpurpose.com -

APPENDIX D
Family Dinner Traditions

CANDLE OF HONOR

Choose one person to honor at dinner each night, by lighting a special candle in front of them. Say why you chose them and then the entire family applauds their greatness before blowing out the flame. Be ready for some tears and upset kids when you first start doing this, because those who are not chosen are obviously disappointed.

The Candle of Honor isn't an "everyone gets a trophy" experience, so don't start lighting candles for all. This is meant to be a teaching moment to show the kids how their turn will eventually come and that we can be happy for others in their times of joy.

HIGHS AND LOWS

As you eat, go around the table and say one great thing about your day and another not so great thing. It encourages everyone to realize that our lives are made up of blessings and hard times. These are great ways to spark conversations too.

As our kids have gotten older, sometimes we change it up and say how we failed that day or how we were a blessing to someone or how someone blessed us. The point is for everyone to have a voice and contribute to the family conversation.

ENCOURAGEMENT FEASTS

We used to do an encouragement feast before we started our family meetings. Go around the table and say "What I love about (the person to your right) is …" It used to be so precious the things our kids would say until the time when one of the boys could not for the life of him come up with anything for his sister, which brought her to tears.

But it was a real moment that brought forward the fact that she hadn't been treating people in our family well, and unfortunately, it's hard to come up with kind, loving things to say about someone who hasn't been showing up virtuous. Good luck playing this heartfelt game with teenagers!

THE TALKING STICK

If you have a big family and everyone seems to talk over one another, you may want to make a family talking stick. Decorate a stick or find something unique during one of your family travels to pass around the table. You are not allowed to talk unless you are in possession of the family talking stick. This way the person who wants to talk can be heard and listened to with respect.

APPENDIX E

Stage-Appropriate Tasks

EVEN TODDLERS CAN HELP WITH THINGS SUCH AS:

Carry in the newspaper or mail.

Wash tables and counters with damp cloth.

Pick up toys and clothes.

Help set the table – napkins, silverware.

Clean up after themselves after meals.

Help put groceries away.

Seal and stamp envelopes.

Assist in picking out their own clothes.

Put own clothes away.

AGES 6–12 APPROPRIATE TASKS

1. **Self-manage entire morning routine**
   Wake up using an alarm clock.
   Make *own* bed.
   Make *own* breakfast and pack school lunch on some days.
   Pack *own* backpack and sports bags.

2. **Help out around the house (a.k.a. chores)**
Do laundry:
   Sort white clothes from dark clothes.
   Help change bedsheets and wash dirty sheets.
   Fold simple laundry items and put them away.
   Match socks.
   Help fold family towels and washcloths.

Clean the house:
   Barney said it best back in the day:
   "Clean up, clean up, everybody everywhere.
   Clean, up, clean up. Everybody do your share."
   Help with vacuuming, sweeping, and dusting.
   Clean bathroom sinks, toilets, and tubs with wipes.
   Empty trash cans around the house.
   Wash dishes, load, and unload dishwasher.
   Push trash and recycling cans to curb.

3. **Make a meal, or two, or three**
   Put groceries away.
   Prepare simple breakfast/lunch and clean up.
   Prepare simple dinners for the family.

4. **Miscellaneous household tasks**
   Wash family car.
   Change batteries and lightbulbs.

Walk, bathe and groom pets.

Organize closet and drawers monthly.

Know how to stamp, address, and mail a letter.

AGES 13–15 APPROPRIATE TASKS

Iron clothes.

Yard work – Mow lawn, rake leaves, spread mulch.

Help with administrative tasks in parents' businesses.

Start their own side business.

Prepare family meals one day a week.

Babysit siblings.

Fill out all paperwork for school, sports, and medical to best of their ability.

AGES 16–18 APPROPRIATE TASKS

Car maintenance – know how to pump and pay for gas; change a tire.

Run errands for the family.

Handle their own checking account.

Know how to pay bills by check.

Know how to appropriately tip waitstaff when out to eat.

Adapted from *The Me, Me, Me Epidemic.*[xxx]

Acknowledgments

There are so many people whom God has used in beautiful ways to influence and encourage my personal journey of motherhood and writing. We were never meant to parent or write alone. It takes a village to raise a child and write a book, and I'm so thankful and humbled by the amazing people the Lord has surrounded me with.

First and foremost, thank you to my husband, Keith, who spent countless hours listening to my ideas and holding down the family fort so that I could write. This book would've never happened without your unconditional love and support.

Thank you to my fearless writing coach and developmental editor Susan Pohlman. I love that our crazy, life-changing family sabbaticals brought us together. Thank you for believing in me and for not letting me give up and go to work at Starbucks when I really wanted to. Your kind heart, innate wisdom, and professional skills helped me more than you will ever know.

Thank you to all of my wonderful friends and family who have encouraged me to keep persevering to write this book. I am humbled by your belief in me, and your friendship is hands down one of God's biggest blessings in my life. My life is forever changed for the better because of each of you.

Thank you to my blog followers for your patience with me getting this book out into the world. Writing a book while raising four children and adopting another in the process has been quite the journey. Thank you for your encouragement and for reading what my heart has to say.

Thank you to John Rosemond for saying yes to writing my foreword which catapulted me to actually finish this book.

Thank you to Joe White for coming alongside Keith and I in our desire to raise faith-filled, God loving children. I can't thank you enough for taking the time to read and endorse my work.

Thank you to Dennis Trittin for being one of my biggest champions along this journey. Your heart for parents, families and fellow writers encourages me regularly.

Thank you to Arlene Pellicane for encouraging me early on to write this book. It's a joy to follow your work and I'm so grateful you took the time to endorse mine.

Thank you to the talented Diana Elizabeth for taking my author photo.

Thank you to my publisher Nicole Gebhardt and the Niche Pressworks team for bringing this project to fruition. It has been a joy collaborating with you to produce this final product. You are a blessing to many!

About the Author

Amy Carney is the founder of Parent on Purpose, an organization created to empower and equip moms and dads throughout the eighteen-year journey of full-time parenthood.

Amy is a former journalist who currently writes about intentional parenting and family life on her blog, www.AmyCarney.com, as well as for various freelance print and online outlets. She is a John Rosemond Leadership Parenting Coach and speaks on stages about parenting on purpose and living a life of impact and meaning.

She is a champion for kids in foster care and is an advocate for AASK (Aid to the Adoption of Special Kids) and National Adoption Day in Maricopa County.

Amy and her retired NHL husband, Keith, are parents to five children—firstborn triplet sons, a subsequent daughter, and their bonus son who joined their family through adoption from foster care in 2016.

Learn more about Amy's work at www.AmyCarney.com and be sure to join her community by signing up for her email newsletter!

parent on purpose
- WITH AMY CARNEY -

Connect with me on social media
@amylcarney

www.amycarney.com

Notes

----

i.   French Cully, Christine, Luba Falk Feigenberg, Ed.D., and Sasha L. Ribic, Psy.D. "The State of the Kid 2017." Highlights.com. 2017. https://www.highlights.com/sites/default/files/public/sotk17_report_final_0.pdf.

ii.   Weissbourd, Rick, and Stephanie Jones. "The Children We Mean to Raise." Making Caring Common. 2014. https://mcc.gse.harvard.edu/the-children-we-mean-to-raise.

iii.   Rogers, Fred. FredRogers.org. https://www.fredrogers.org/about/beginnings/.

iv.   Brown, Brene. *Brené Brown, Daring Greatly: How the Courage to Be Vulnerable Transforms the Way We Live, Love, Parent, and Lead.* New York, NY: Penguin Group, 2012.

v.   Rosemond, John. Leadership Parent Coaching Retreat, North Carolina, New Bern, June 2018.

vi.   Hammond, Darell. Play Deprivation: 5 Solutions to a Weighty Problem. November 11, 2011. https://www.huffingtonpost.com/darell-hammond/play-deprivation-5-soluti_b_244343.html.

vii.   Sutton-Smith, Brian. National Institute for Play. http://www.nifplay.org.

viii.   Website Banner Quote Brown, Stuart, MD. "National Institute for Play Facebook Post." June 15, 2016. https://www.facebook.com/National-Institute-for-Play-104024156305741/.

ix.   Entin, Esther. "All Work and No Play: Why Your Kids Are More Anxious, Depressed." The Atlantic.com. October 12, 2011.

https://www.theatlantic.com/health/archive/2011/10/all-work-and-no-play-why-your-kids-are-more-anxious-depressed/246422/.

x.   Keller, Dana. *Play and Social Change: Reframing Play as a Lifelong Activity.* Report. Social and Pedagogy, Arizona State University.

xi.   Turkle, Sherry. *Reclaiming Conversation: The Power of Talk in a Digital Age.* NY, NY: Penguin Books, 2016.

xii.   Strohman, Lisa, Dr. *Unplug: Raising Kids In a Technology Addicted World.* AZ, 2015.

xiii. Lynum, Erin. 936 *Pennies: Discovering the Joy of Intentional Parenting.* Baker Publishing Group, 2018.

xiv.   Campos, Lorle. *Happy Home.* Once Upon A Family Publishing, 2008.

xv.   "2010 Family Dinners Report Finds: Teens Who Have Infrequent Dinners Likelier to Expect to Use Drugs in the Future." PRNewswire. com. September 22, 2010. https://www.prnewswire.com/news-releases/2010-family-dinners-report-finds-teens-who-have-infrequent-family-dinners-likelier-to-expect-to-use-drugs-in-the-future-103499414. html.

xvi.   Carney, Amy. "Stop Doing These 8 Things for Your Teen This School Year." AmyCarney.com. https://amycarney.com/walk-away-from-doing-these-8-things-for-your-teen-this-school-year/.

xvii. Chalk-Wadsworth, Phoebe, associate athletic director and professor in the sports management undergraduate program at University of Arizona, in discussion with the author, December 2017.

xviii. Nelson, Margaret, vice dean of Barrett Honors College at Arizona State University in discussion with the author, December 2017.

xix.   Lahey, Jessica. *The Gift of Failure: How the Best Parents Learn to Let Go so Their Children Can Succeed.* New York, NY: Harper Collins Publishers, 2015.

xx.   Gilboa, Deborah, Dr. "Key Responsibilities EVERY Child Should Know How to Shoulder." Interview. AFineParent.com. May 7, 2018. https://afineparent.com/positive-parenting-conference

xxi.   Nelson, Margaret, vice dean of Barrett Honors College at Arizona State University in discussion with the author, December 2017.

xxii. McRaven, Admiral William H. "University of Texas at Austin 2014 Commencement Address" https://youtu.be/pxBQLFLei70

xxiii. Apodaca, Alex, Chief Operating Officer & CJO First Cup, LLC, in discussion with the author, January 2018.

xxiv. DeSilver, Drew. "The Share of Teens with Summer Jobs Has Plunged since 2000, and the Type of Work They Do Has Shifted." Pewresearch. org. July 2, 2018. https://pewrsr.ch/2MIlf63.

xxv. "Dictionary by Merriam-Webster: America's Most-trusted Online Dictionary." Merriam-Webster. Accessed October 24, 2018. https://www.merriam-webster.com/.

xxvi. Wynn, Max. "Marian Wright Edelman Delivers Stirring Speech." Luskin. ucla.edu. December 6, 2013. https://luskin.ucla.edu/marian-wright-edelman-delivers-stirring-speech/.

xxvii. Stone, Dave. *How to Raise Selfless Kids in a Self-centered World.* Nashville, TN: Thomas Nelson, 2012.

xxviii. Munsey, Phil. *Legacy Now.* Lake Mary, FL: Charisma House, 2008.

xxix. Carney, Amy. "You Are Dying. Live like It." AmyCarney.com. January 2017. https://amycarney.com/you-are-dying-live-like-it/.

xxx. McCready, Amy. The "Me, Me, Me, Epidemic A Step-by-Step Guide To Raising Capable, Grateful Kids in an Over-Entitled World. New York, NY: Tarcher Perigee, 2015.

Made in the USA
Las Vegas, NV
11 May 2022

48757901R10075